Dostoevsky

Dostoevsky

Richard Freeborn

HAUS PUBLISHIN

First published in Great Britain in 2003 by
Haus Publishing Limited
26 Cadogan Court
Draycott Avenue
London SW3 3BX

A CIP catalogue record for this book
is available from the British Library

ISBN 1-904341-276

Typeset by Lobster Design

Printed and bound by Graphicom in Vicenza, Italy

Front cover: portrait of Dostoevsky, by Perov © courtesy of Topham
Picturepoint
Back cover: portrait of Dostoevsky, by Favorsky © courtesy of Novosti

Contents

Preface 1

Becoming a Man 3

From *Poor Folk* to Penal Servitude 20

Siberia and Silence 37

From *Time* to the Underground 49

Crime and Punishment 63

Second Exile. *The Idiot* 80

The Devils 92

Return to Russia 108

The Brothers Karamazov 117

Final Triumph 130

Notes 138

Chronology 148

Further Reading 154

Picture Sources 157

Index 158

About the author 167

Preface

Dostoevsky is known as the author of the great nineteenth-century Russian novels *Crime and Punishment*, *The Idiot*, *The Devils* (or *The Possessed*) and *The Brothers Karamazov*. This short study is intended as a guide to his life as a writer and an examination of his literary achievement in the context of his time. It is intended for the general reader and avoids technical or specialist terms wherever possible.

All the translations are my own and based on definitive Russian texts. In transliterating Russian names I have chosen to use such common Anglicized forms as 'Dostoevsky', for instance, rather than 'Dostoevskii', 'Tolstoy' rather than 'Tolstoi' and 'Marsha' rather than 'Masha'. In cases where 'e' is pronounced 'yo' in proper names the change has been noted in brackets at the first instance, e.g. Fedor (pron. F*yo*dor). Otherwise, in all transliterations of titles or quotations I have tried to follow the Library of Congress system.

Due to the compression needed for such a short study many details have not received the amplification they deserve in dealing with such a complex writer. Readers seeking more information are referred to the Further Reading section, but no one who writes about Dostoevsky can afford to overlook the masterly edition of the Collected Works published in the Soviet Union between 1972 and 1990 (*Polnoe sobranie sochinenii v 30 tomakh*), nor the virtually definitive study of his life and works by Joseph Frank that has been appearing, volume by volume, since 1977 and is completed with the fifth volume in 2002. It is an honour to be able to acknowledge with deep gratitude the breadth and scholarship of these undertakings and to confess a whole-hearted indebtedness to both in composing this short study.

I would also like to express my gratitude to Barbara Schwepcke for commissioning it. Warm thanks are also due to Nigel Jones, historian and biographer of Rupert Brooke, for suggesting it. Above all, I am grateful to my wife, Anne, for bearing with it and sacrificing a summer holiday for its sake.

RICHARD FREEBORN

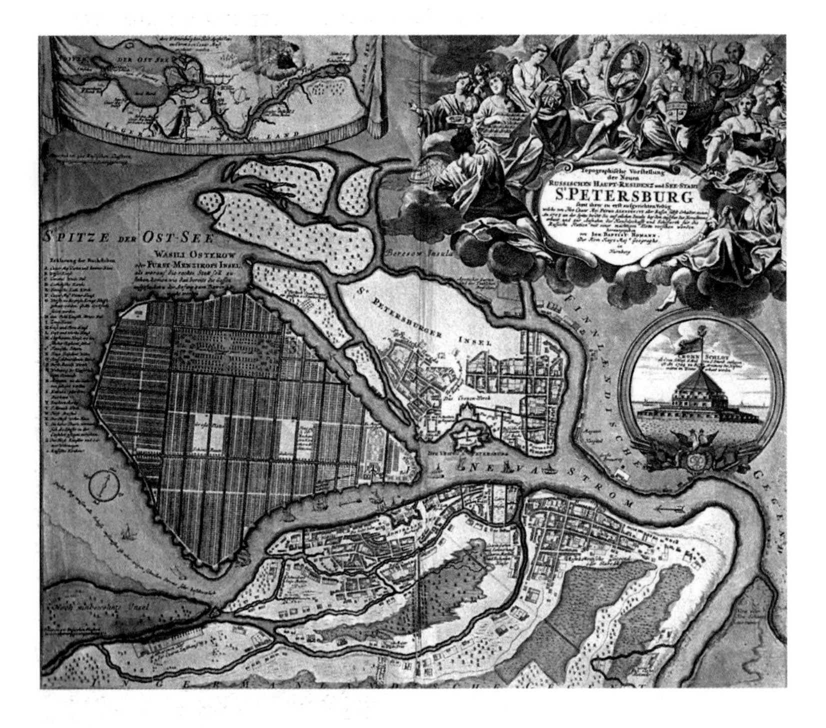

Becoming a man

Dostoevsky was born into an empire as big as the moon. In 1821, the year of his birth, the Russian empire occupied territory equivalent to the surface area of the face of the moon, according to Humboldt, the famous explorer. As the greatest Russian novelist of the nineteenth century – rivalled only by Tolstoy in terms of achievement and influence – Dostoevsky's reputation has an equivalent dimension of greatness in its command of a multitude of human attitudes, from the most saintly to the most pathological, the deepest emotional states to the most perversely criminal, the greatest sense of evil to the most sublime belief in a Christian God. It cannot be emphasized too much, however, that he was never divorced from the realities of the Russian world into which he was born.

Count Leo Nikolaevich Tolstoy (1828–1910) is best remembered for *War and Peace* (*Vonya i mir*, 1863–9) and his second great work, *Anna Karenina* (1874–6). A spiritual crisis in 1879 led him towards a form of Christian anarchism. He dressed as a peasant, became a vegetarian pacifist, repudiated his former works and divided his property among his family. He caught a chill and died in a siding of a railway station.

Chekhov and Tolstoy

The Russian empire at his birth had achieved a peak of influence and success with the defeat of the Napoleonic invasion of Russia in 1812 and the triumphant entry of Russian troops into Paris in 1814. In the nineteenth century Russia was never to enjoy greater military triumph or greater international influence, but there was to be no Russian participation in the final defeat of Napoleon at Waterloo and the rest of the century was to witness a gradual erosion of Russia's role *vis-à-vis* Europe.

The better educated among the class of noblemen who were officers of the victorious Russian troops that entered Paris could not fail to acknowledge the difference between their own heritage of autocracy and the democratic principles, however limited, evident among the vanquished. The contrast served to stimulate the need to achieve some of the Western freedoms that had been promised by Tsar Alexander I (1777–1825) when he first ascended the throne in 1801. Although Alexander himself became increasingly conservative and religious in his convictions after 1815, the nobility of a Moscow largely destroyed by fire during the Napoleonic invasion sought in rebuilding it to 'Europeanize' and 'Frenchify' their urban palaces.

Tsar Alexander I 1830

European fashions, already fostered in the eighteenth century by the policies of Peter the Great (1672–1725), became a major invasive element in Russian life despite the hostility to Napoleon. In a cultural and ideological sense, the greatest European challenge

Serfdom. Ilya Repin's painting, Bargehaulers on the Volga, 1870

to Russian conservatism was offered by Romanticism, particularly the aspect represented by the English poet Lord Byron (1788–1824) and his cult of the free individual who aspired to be master of his own destiny. Such a new image of man had, of course, a darker, Frankenstein side that asserted a right to defy divine law and set humanity free from the shackles of church morality. This influence, like Romanticism itself, could travel across national borders more easily than armies. Simultaneously, on the economic and social front, as if it were a Frankenstein's monster unloosed upon Russia, came the Industrial Revolution, the beginnings of a capitalist economy and the growth of an increasingly numerous entrepreneurial merchant class.

Almost as a bulwark against such change, and most certainly as an impediment to it, was the fact of serfdom upon which the socio-economic and political structure of Russian society was based. This structure was bolstered by the Orthodox Church and the vested interest of a serf-owning nobility. The Russian empire at the time of Dostoevsky's birth was in many ways a semi-feudal hierarchy dominated by a Tsar who relied on a hereditary nobility, numbering less than 100,000, to govern or oversee a landed

A serf was an unfree peasant bound to the land he worked, paying the lord of the manor a fee and providing service in return for protection and the use of his land. While serfdom declined in Western Europe in the late Middle Ages, it was not abolished in Eastern Europe until the nineteenth century.

peasant population numbering many millions, who could be bought and sold, punished and conscripted into the army more or less at their masters' whim. The injustice of this situation gradually sapped the supposed strength of Russia and its imperial aspirations.

This is not to deny that the Russian empire continued to increase throughout the nineteenth century by a slow process of reducing Turkish influence in the Balkans and colonial expansion beyond the Caucasus and in Central Asia. When such expansionism met serious opposition and defeat – as, for instance, in the Crimean War (1854–5) – the government attempted to initiate reforms, but these (especially the emancipation of the serfs in 1861) tended to look like long-overdue concessions to the need for change rather than modernization along Western lines. In many respects, nineteenth-century Russia had features characteristic of a Third World country ruled dictatorially by a government always finding time unripe for change. The outcome was inevitable.

There emerged by degrees a thinking minority opposed to the Government. In its social complexion, as in its degrees of opposition, it differed from generation to generation, but no matter how thoughtful and even patriotic it might be, government reaction to it was always hostile. Broadly speaking, this minority became known as the Russian intelligentsia. To consider the intelligentsia as having no other purpose than opposition would be unfair, yet the rigidity of official attitudes to all forms of dissent always involved repression, censorship, imprisonment and exile, or, in extreme cases, death. The first major instance of such dissent occurred in 1825, when Dostoevsky was barely four years old.

The Decembrist Revolt (so-called because it took place in

The failed insurrection of the Decembrists on Senate Square, St Petersburg. 14 December 1825. Watercolour by K I Kolman

December 1825) was a deliberate attempt by officers of the leading guards' regiments in St Petersburg to force the autocracy to make political concessions. The event occurred hastily, without due planning, as a result of the sudden death of Alexander I in Taganrog on the Volga. A period of interregnum ensued in St Petersburg before his brother, Nicholas I (1795–1855), ascended the throne rather than Grand-Duke Constantine, the presumed heir. Although certain plans had been laid by the leading members of the northern and southern societies that formed the nucleus of the Decembrist movement, the uncertainty at the heart of government during the interregnum seemed fortuitous and, on the morning when troops quartered in the capital were to swear allegiance to the new Tsar, the dissident officers marched their regiments on to the Senate Square shouting for 'Constantine and Constitution!' (the latter – *konstitutsia* – thought to be a reference to Constantine's wife). There was a stand-off. Finally Nicholas summoned up the courage to order cannon to fire on the insurgents and many were driven into the Neva River and drowned. Although the revolt ended in the course of a short winter's day, its consequences, like the cannon-fire, reverberated for the remaining 30 years of Nicholas I's reign.

To the autocracy the Decembrist Revolt seemed an act of treasonable disloyalty by the Russian nobility towards their sovereign, exacerbated by the role of guards' officers in the insurgency. Five of the ringleaders were hanged and as many as 100 participants and their relatives were dispatched into Siberian exile. The shock of such disloyalty led Nicholas I to institute what was called a Third Department, virtually a secret police designed to aid in the investigation and suppression of all forms of dissent throughout the empire. It became notorious as an arm of government in persecuting all forms of freedom of thought, particularly in the sphere of literature.

During the late 1830s and the 1840s literature assumed an importance in Russian life far greater than it enjoyed in Western Europe. Despite official censorship, it acquired a role, whether through the medium of journals or *belles-lettres*, both educational and instrumental in spreading new ideas, influencing opinion and offering up a mirror to reality. Were it not for the pervasive initial influence of the writer Alexander Pushkin, whose work first became popular and widely read in the 1820s, literary standards might not have been as exacting as they were, for there can be little doubt that his example in introducing so many new styles and genres to Russian literature enormously enhanced the range of poetic tastes. By stealth, as it were, an informed readership evolved under his influence. The Sentimentalism of the late eighteenth century blended with the Classicism of the period to make the 'freedoms' of Romanticism seem especially startling to Russian sensibilities. In Pushkin's hands they came to reflect a particular form of Byronism and expressed themselves most obviously in the portrayal of types of hero and heroine typical of growing Russian social self-consciousness.

Pushkin's first disillusioned Byronic hero was the Russian officer depicted in his long poem 'The Prisoner of the Caucasus' (*Kavkazskii plennik*, 1822), designed, as he claimed, to demonstrate 'the indifference to life and its pleasures, the premature ageing of the soul' of the youth of the nineteenth century.[1] Pushkin felt that this initial attempt was unsuccessful in its aim of depicting a Romantic type, but as the Romantic treatment grew less marked in his work he offered, in portraying Aleko in 'The Gypsies' (*Tsygany*, 1824), a study of a supposedly civilized man who sought freedom among 'noble savages', only to find his conscience suborned by his own murderous instincts which left him ultimately an outcast and superfluous in society. Simultaneously, and on a much larger scale, Pushkin was developing his portrayal of a much more realistic type, that of his most memorable creation, the St Petersburg dandy Eugene Onegin of the eponymous eight-part 'novel in verse' (1823–31).

Inspired by Byron's *Don Juan* (1819–24), the portrait that emerged embraced not merely

Moscow-born poet, novelist and dramatist Alexander Pushkin (1799–1837) was exiled to the southern provinces in 1820 for his revolutionary political verse. There he began a sophisticated novel in verse, *Eugene Onegin* (1833). In 1824 he was transferred to north-west Russia where he wrote the great historical drama *Boris Godunov* (1831). He returned to Moscow in 1826 and was killed in a duel.

Alexander Pushkin 1827

the urban background of the hero and his disillusionment, but also the rural world of Russia and his relationship with a heroine, Tatiana, who, if infatuated with what she supposed were his Romantic heroic traits, gradually and heartbrokenly came to understand his true nature beneath the dandyish pose. As much dramatic as lyrical in its evocation of the Russian world of the early nineteenth century, Pushkin's masterpiece highlighted in its climax the tragedy of a relationship doomed by social norms, cultural difference and moral sanction from ever becoming the true love and happiness that hero and heroine could have enjoyed. If Onegin coldly rejected Tatiana when she, in her rural innocence, professed her love for him, she ultimately rejected him when the tables were turned and he fell in love with a Tatiana transformed into a stately beauty of the St Petersburg *beau monde*. Even if he may have seemed 'superfluous', a cold egoist who found his heart irrevocably pierced by a love experienced too late, of the several ironies in his situation among the most interesting was the very calendar of events governing his supposed life.

For if one assumes that Pushkin's fiction had, in its presumption of realism, a degree of historical verisimilitude, the dating of Onegin's life can be shown to relate to a period prior to 1825.[2] Could this mean that he might redeem himself and perhaps give meaning to his life by becoming associated with those, like the Decembrists, who wished to change Russia, achieve constitutional reform, abolish the injustice of serfdom and create a more egalitarian society? The question is not entirely rhetorical. Russian literature was the only forum in Russian life where such implicitly revolutionary ideas could receive an airing, however covertly, and where anything like an answer could be found. It was to this literary legacy that Dostoevsky was born in 1821.

*

According to church records, he was born on 30 October 1821 (O S)[3] at the Hospital for the Poor in Moscow and christened Fedor Mikhailovich, second son of Dr Mikhail Dostoevsky, chief medical director of the hospital.

Maria Dostoevsky by Popov 1823

Dr Dostoevsky had earlier been an army surgeon. His presence at the battle of Borodino (1812), the single most important engagement of the Napoleonic invasion of Russia, had introduced him to the medical horrors of the battlefield. By experience, then, as well as by temperament, he had a reputation as a severe, rather hard-bitten, short-tempered man, though disciplined and efficient. In social terms he may have been less privileged than his wife Maria (born Nechaeva), who came from an old merchant family that had fallen on hard times as a result of the Napoleonic invasion. She was more cultured than her husband and generally exerted a more loving and intellectually stimulating influence on a family that grew rapidly from two boys to a third, Andrei, and then three more surviving children, Vera, Nikolai and Alexandra.

Mikhail Dostoevsky by Popov 1823

Dostoevsky was only a year younger than his brother Mikhail and shared a room with him in the cramped quarters of the apartment, first to the right of the hospital's main entrance and later to the left, where the Dostoevsky museum is now housed. His father made great efforts to ensure that his children were insulated from the hospital world, but of course they were never able to escape the sights of sickness and poverty around them. In any case, the situation of the Hospital for the Poor was hardly attractive. It was on the site of a morgue and close to an assembly point for prisoners on the way to Siberia. These facts of Dostoevsky's boyhood can be easily judged as ironic markers for his destiny and must have had an effect on his psyche. To exaggerate them would be to misjudge the more powerful influence exerted by his father.

Dr Dostoevsky had ambitions for his children. He wished to achieve noble status and therefore set about teaching his eldest sons Latin as a subject befitting children of the nobility. Although he never resorted to physical violence, these sessions were memorable for the father's short temper. There can be no denying that for Dostoevsky the father–son relationship became of supreme importance. It is mirrored in his fiction from his earliest work to his last, but allied to it was an abiding sensitivity about social position, an intense nervous awareness of slights and insults and a seemingly arrogant insistence on individual dignity. The father did indeed achieve entitlement to nobility rank in 1828 and was therefore able to purchase a small estate in the Tula region centred on the village of Darovoe. This became the young Dostoevsky's first opportunity to see the world beyond the confines of the hospital and to acquaint himself, however superficially, with the life of the peasantry.

From his mother, on the other hand, he learned about the Bible. The Dostoevsky household was religious. Deep and abiding faith acquired at his mother's knee involved knowledge of the lives of the saints as well as regular family prayers, church visits and pilgrimages to local monasteries. The single most important lesson

Dostoevsky learned in his boyhood was belief in a compassionate and loving Christ, the saviour of the world. By degrees this messianic vision fastened itself into his imagination and became transmuted into an image of Russian national identity as an icon of hope for all mankind.

His mother's compassionate interest in her children found expression also in her management of the small Tula estate. The peasants loved her for her caring nature and were glad to have her as their new mistress, just as among the most lyrical and touching episodes in Dostoevsky's works are those drawn from his boyhood memories of summer holidays in the countryside. The extent to which he, very much a child of an urban environment and its accompanying squalor, became truly aware of the depth of peasant hardship must always be open to doubt. He played with peasant children, organized games and left behind a vivid portrait of a chance acquaintance with a 50-year-old peasant called Marei, who comforted him after the boy had been scared by someone warning of a wolf in the locality. Dostoevsky forgot the encounter, only to be reminded of the peasant's kindliness some 20 years later while in penal servitude when he most needed such comfort, or as he put it in *The Diary of a Writer* for 1876: *In Siberia I recalled that meeting with such clarity, right down to the last detail. I mean it settled into my soul unnoticed, of its own accord and without my willing it and I suddenly remembered it when I needed to; I remembered the kindly, motherly smile of the poor peasant serf, his crossing himself and shaking his head and saying: 'There, don't you be afraid, little one!' And I particularly remembered his thick finger, covered in soil, which he softly and with shy tenderness placed on my quivering lips.*[4]

That finger covered in soil can be said to mark the beginnings of what became for Dostoevsky a philosophy of the soil (*pochvennichestvo*). The memory evoked a sense of Christian charity uniquely characteristic, in his opinion, of the oppressed Russian peasantry. This was a gift it could offer to the intelligentsia and from which the intelligentsia should learn, as Dostoevsky later insisted, but more significantly it identified for him the true spirit of Russia.

As a boy, though, there were other matters upon which Dostoevsky's imagination could feed and which would remain with him as lifelong influences. A visit to the theatre to see Schiller's *The Robbers*, for example, or family reading sessions when he was first introduced to the classics of Russian literature, particularly Pushkin, or his fascination with the Gothic horrors of Ann Radcliffe – all these formed a legacy that enriched his ability to dream and transform such dreams into raw material for his later development as a writer.

Friedrich von Schiller (1759–1805) published his first play, *The Robbers* (*Die Räuber*, 1781), at his own expense, but it was an instant success due to its anarchic subject matter. He went on to write his most famous dramas *Wallenstein* (1798–99), *Maria Stuart* (1800), *The Maid of Orleans* (*Die Jungfrau von Orleans*, 1801) and *William Tell* (*Wilhelm Tell*, 1804).

As for education in a more formal sense, for Dostoevsky and his brother Mikhail it began early, first at home, then at a school run by a certain Druzhakov and in 1834 at the Chermak boarding school where education was of a high standard and had a bias towards literary subjects. The school experience was reflected, not very favourably but probably truthfully, in the young Arkady Dolgoruky's schooldays at the Touchard school in *An Accidental Family* (*Podrostok*, 1875).[5]

Dostoevsky received as good an education as could have been expected at the time. Chiefly, he learned to educate himself through reading. It would be wrong to assume he was deprived intellectually as a boy; nor should it be thought that his childhood

Ann Radcliffe (1764–1823) published several Gothic novels, including *The Mysteries of Udolpho* (1794) and *The Italian* (1797). They were extremely successful and much imitated at the time, which prompted Jane Austen (1775–1817) to write her satire *Northanger Abbey* (1818).

The Flour Bridge over the Yekaterinsky Canal, St Petersburg by Boris Smelov

was harsh. In general, he remembered it with pleasure, but it was circumscribed by poverty, epitomized by the Hospital for the Poor, and it concluded with the tragedy of his mother's death from tuberculosis in February 1837. This event marked the end of family life as such, just as for the two eldest Dostoevsky brothers it marked the end of Moscow life. Within a few months of their mother's death they were dispatched to St Petersburg to gain entrance to the most prestigious military academy in the country, the Academy for Engineers.

The journey to St Petersburg began with a moment of horrifying epiphany. At a post-station *en route* Dostoevsky witnessed an act of gratuitous violence when a government courier hastily knocked back a couple of vodkas, jumped into his carriage and showered down a rain of blows on his wretched peasant driver who in turn whipped his horses into a frenzy. This moment – as well as the unforgettable picture of a peasant beating his horse to death in Raskolnikov's dream at the opening of *Crime and Punishment*

Mikhail Dostoevsky by Trutovsky

(1867) – was Dostoevsky's initiation into the reality of a life based on the violent subjection of the weak to the strong. St Petersburg itself was to embody in its imposing Western-style architecture and ramrod-straight streets the right to employ such violence at will in its subjection of Russia to its imperial power. This world and the violent subculture that it generated came to fascinate Dostoevsky. He became its principal literary interpreter.

Both brothers received intense coaching for admission to the Academy once they had reached St Petersburg, but only Dostoevsky gained a place. Mikhail was refused on health grounds and had to content himself with the less prestigious Academy in Tallinn. One happy result of this has been the survival of a number of deeply revealing letters from Dostoevsky to his brother describing his personal and cultural evolution during his years at the Academy of Engineers. He may have made one or two friends, but to none, it seems, did he open himself as candidly as he did to his brother. One friend, Ivan Shidlovsky, five years his senior, appeared to represent the ideal essence of Romanticism in human terms and impressed Dostoevsky by his belief in God, his worship of the arts and his purity of soul. For all that, Dostoevsky appears to have preferred his own company and became renowned among his peer group for his reclusive lifestyle at the Academy.

He was beset by money problems. His letters to his father begging for additional funds testified often to his need to match the expenditure of wealthier classmates. His father, it seems, made every effort to meet these requests for money, hard-pressed though he was at this time. To justify himself, Dostoesvky went to some lengths in his letters to describe his progress with as much artfulness as possible in endeavouring to conceal his weakness as a mathematician or his poor showing in such an essential military subject as topography. He showed a talent for drawing that was to stay with him for the rest of his life, as so many of his surviving manuscripts demonstrate with their sketches of Gothic arches and other architectural profiles. It was to literature and his private reading that he devoted most effort. His letters to his brother contain salvoes of names fired off with enthusiastic gusto ranging from Shakespeare (1564–1616) – especially *Hamlet* (1602) – to Jean Racine (1639–99), Pierre Corneille (1606–84), Blaise Pascal (1623–62), E T W Hoffmann (1776–1822), Honoré de Balzac (1799–1850), Johann Wolfgang von Goethe (1749–1832), Victor Hugo (1802–85) and George Sand (1804–76). Along with such an apparently encyclopedic knowledge (remarkable in any case despite the fact that it was no doubt the product of enthusiastic dilettantism rather than close study), he also fired off, with characteristic adolescent precocity, his 'sad ideas' about the nature of humanity and in so doing offered assumptions fundamental to his future work: *Only one condition of things is it given to man to know: the atmosphere of his soul consists of a fusion of heaven and earth; what a disobedient child is man; the law of spiritual nature is broken . . . It seems to me that this world of ours is a purgatory of heavenly spirits, darkened by sinful thought. It seems to me that the world has acquired a negative meaning and out of an elevated, elegant spirituality has come forth satire.*[6]

The vision of humanity as a battlefield of contraries, of *pro* and *contra*, of the world as a purgatory which is potentially a paradise, but darkened by sinful thought and, that most grotesque of contrarieties, in which the highest spiritual strivings can emerge as parody or satire of the spiritual way, was a vision to be explored by Dostoevsky from the beginning to the end of his life.

A further and equally significant instance occurred in his letter of 31 October 1838 when he asked his brother what he meant by the word 'know': *To know nature, the soul, God, love ... These things are known by the heart not by the mind.* [...] *The conductor of thought through the transitory envelope* [of the flesh] *into the vessel of the soul is the* mind. *The mind is a material faculty . . . The soul or the spirit lives by the thought that the heart whispers to it . . . Thought is born in the soul. The mind is an instrument, a machine, driven by the fires of the spirit.*[7]

From the ultra-Romantic obscurity of these statements certain significant and rather startling notions emerge, such as the emphasis placed upon the materialization of the mind, its embodiment as an instrument or machine. The relationship between soul, mind and heart offered here has the effect of demonstrating the principle determining the role which ideas have to play in 'possessing' Dostoevsky's heroes, acting upon them infectiously and pathologically.

In his own case, few things acted upon him as gravely as did the death of his father. After his wife's death, Dr Dostoevsky had retired to the village of Darovoe on his small Tula estate where he became depressed, drank, womanized and antagonized his peasants. On 6 June 1839 he suddenly died and within a short time it was rumoured that his peasants had murdered him. Had he in fact been killed? Or could his death be construed as a form of patricide?

The question has been much debated. Sigmund Freud's version stipulated patricide by proxy.[8] Dostoevsky desired the death of his father on the pattern of Ivan Karamazov's claim that 'We all desire the death of our father', and the resulting emotional conflict between vengeance and guilt, along with the supposed evidence for an Oedipus complex precipitated Dostoevsky's first epileptic seizure. The evidence for this interpretation is subject to considerable doubt. It is now generally assumed that Dr

Dostoevsky died most likely from apoplexy (*kondrashka* 'with an aura', as he himself called it), not at the hands of his peasants. That it may have been a form of epilepsy is possible, although there is no evidence to justify the assertion that news of his father's death caused Dostoevsky to have an epileptic fit. The affliction could very likely have been hereditary, however. Dostoevsky later feared as much when his three-year-old son, Aleksei, died from a prolonged attack in 1878.[9]

Freud's attempt to attribute the epileptic condition to hysteria probably over-dramatizes the gravity of Dostoevsky's reaction to news of his father's death. The effect was certainly lasting, of that there can be no doubt, since patricide became a preoccupation of his to the end of his life. It is hardly very remarkable that in the first extant letter after the event he confessed to his brother that he had shed copious tears over their father's death. Grandiloquently, naturally, he went on to explain his own condition at the time and produced towards the letter's conclusion a remarkably mature statement of his primary intention in life. It can be regarded as a 17-year-old's epigraph to his career and purpose as a writer:

My soul is not subject to my former violent upsets. All is calm within it, as in the heart of a man who has harboured a deep mystery; to learn 'what life and man means' – I am being reasonably successful in this; I can study characters from the writers with whom the best part of my life is passed in joy and freedom; I can say no more about myself. I am sure of myself. Man is a mystery. The mystery must be solved, and if you spend your whole life trying to solve it, then don't say you have wasted your time; I am preoccupied with this mystery because I wish to be a man.[10]

From *Poor Folk* to Penal Servitude

Dostoevsky's desire to solve the mystery of man became inseparable from his need to solve the mystery of St Petersburg. As a writer he achieved his first outstanding and virtually overnight success through peering at the human truth concealed beneath Peter the Great's creation on the banks of the Neva. No other writer ever captured the 'fantastic' reality of the city better than Dostoevsky and nowhere did he describe the dualism of that urban world better than in a feuilleton he wrote for the first number of his first journal, *Time* (*Vremia*).[11] It seemed to echo the theme of the 17-year-old boy wishing to be a man:

I am passionate about mysteries. I fantasize, I am a mystic and I admit to you that St Petersburg has always seemed something of a mystery. Ever since boyhood, almost lost and abandoned in St Petersburg, I have always been a bit frightened of it. I remember one episode, which had nothing special about it but which gave me a terrible shock. I will tell it you in every detail; yet it wasn't even an episode, just an impression. But I fantasize, you see, I'm a mystic!

I remember once, on a wintry January evening, I was hurrying home to the Vyborg side. I was very young then. Approaching the Neva, I stopped a moment and threw a keen glance along the length of the river into the smoky, frost-dark distance that had suddenly turned crimson in the last purple rays of a sunset glimmering on the misty horizon. Night was settling over the city and the entire vast surface of the Neva swollen with frozen snow was sprinkled by final flecks of sunlight with endless myriads of sparkling ice needles. There was 20 degrees of frost . . .Freezing steam rose from the tired horses and rushing people. The taut air quivered from the least sound and, as if they were giants, there rose into the cold sky from the roofs on both embankments pillars of smoke that wound and

Snow falling on the Neva in St Petersburg

unwound in their upward progress so that it seemed new buildings formed above the old ones, a new city was building in the air . . . It seemed finally that this entire world, with all its inhabitants, the strong and the weak, with all its dwellings, the hovels of the poor or the gilded palaces, resembled at this twilight hour a fantastic and wonderful mirage, a dream which in its turn would suddenly vanish and evaporate into the dark-blue sky. A strange thought suddenly struck me. I gave a start and my heart was filled at that instant with a burning rush of blood suddenly brought to boiling point by the access of a very powerful but until then unfamiliar feeling. It was as if I realized at that moment something that had been stirring within me but was not yet understood; as if I had seen through to something new, to a completely new world, unfamiliar to me and known only through certain dark rumours, certain mysterious signs. I think that from that moment my existence began . . .[12]

Some significant part of Dostoevsky's genius can be discerned from this passage. His semi-mystical insight into the urban mystery as well as the romance blending into and enhancing the

Mikhail Lermontov

Nikolay Gogol

Vissarion Belinsky

realism of the description are characteristic of his power as a writer to reveal the instant, to penetrate reality and simultaneously 'confess himself', as so many of his heroes were to confess themselves. Claims that he wrote badly, that his style was slipshod by comparison with Turgenev's or Tolstoy's, are seriously challenged when set against such a passage. His style, like the man, could be journalistic, ambiguous, hurried and unconcerned with niceties; it never lacked power, however unstudied, or honesty, however inelegant.

When his existence as a writer began, he was to demonstrate most of all his power as a voice artist, a literary impersonator. At the beginning of the 1840s Russian literature was dominated by three figures: Mikhail Yur'evich Lermontov (1814–41), Nikolay Vasilievich Gogol (1809–52) and Vissarion Grigorevich Belinsky (1811–48). Psychological portraiture was what Lermontov offered in his novel *A Hero of Our Time* (*Geroi nashego vremeni*, 1841), satire was Gogol's contribution in his *Dead Souls* (*Mertvye dushi*, 1842) and Belinsky, the leading critic of the age, offered a vision of literature as the scourge of social injustice. In Belinsky's interpretation, both Lermontov and Gogol had performed an invaluable service in depicting inadequacies in Russian society, whether it be the latter-day Byronic type of Pechorin in Lermontov's case or the venal Chichikov in *Dead Souls* who makes a picaresque journey through Russia in search of dead serfs. The Lermontov version may have highlighted the problem of what became known as the 'superfluous man', but the Gogol version, in its satirical portrayal of types of grotesque landowner, revealed by implication the fundamental injustice of serfdom. Censorship, of course, forbade direct reference, and Belinsky could not point directly to what Gogol's masterpiece so obviously portrayed, but a reading public could easily pick up the hints and, largely through Belinsky's criticism in the leading journal of the decade, Kraevsky's *Fatherland Notes* (*Otechestvennye zapiski*), such a public quickly evolved. In the course of the 1840s Belinsky sought to promote what he called the 'natural school', meaning a literature devoted to depicting Russian reality, and the accolade of founding this school he awarded to Gogol.

Gogol's greatest contribution to the movement was a long short story, *The Overcoat* (*Shinel'*, 1842), about a poor government copying clerk, Akaky Akakievich Bashmachkin, who assiduously saved up to buy a new overcoat, only for it to be stolen from him when he finally got to wear it. The theft led to a desperate search culminating in his death and transforming him into a menacing phantom in a nightmarishly unreal St Petersburg. Narrated in Gogol's magnificently ornamented, uniquely discursive and burlesque manner, *The Overcoat* encapsulated the inhumanly small life of the copying clerk, his momentary discovery of an identity in his brand-new coat and his pitiful attempt to avenge himself on a world that could steal from him his only helpmate in life, his supposed wife, his very soul, as it were. It was out from under Gogol's *Overcoat* that Dostoevsky is said to have claimed he and other Russian writers sprang.

In fact, he emerged from some half-dozen years of study at the Academy of Engineers where, if he did not exactly learn to write, he learned essential powers of discipline and concentration.

Dostoevsky at twenty-six, 1847

Obtaining his discharge from the Academy in 1844, Dostoevsky set about becoming a writer. His earliest ambition, it seems, was to make a name for himself as a playwright and he chose for this purpose themes related to Pushkin's *Boris Godunov* and Schiller's *Maria Stuart*. Impressed, though, by Balzac's visit to St Petersburg in 1843, he abandoned such grandiose historical subjects in favour of a translation of the French novelist's *Eugénie Grandet* (1833).

Dostoevsky's translation was more a version than an exact replica of the French. In any case, this mattered less than the achievement of first publication and the sense that he now had a vocation. He had many different apartments in St Petersburg once free of the Academy, but it was while sharing with Grigorovich, a similarly budding writer, that he began his first original work, *Poor Folk* (*Bednye liudi*, 1846). Long periods, day and night, were spent silently composing at his desk. Secretive and sensitive about his work, he revised this story again and again, though such intense concern for style and finish was not strictly speaking characteristic of him. He loved privacy and was obsessive about it. It contributed to his reputation for unsociability, perhaps also to his impracticality in handling money and perhaps also gave rise to a compensating, often impulsive and misplaced generosity.

Grigorovich had no idea what Dostoevsky had been writing.

When he heard that the poet and editor Nekrasov was looking for contributions for a new publication, he showed him Dostoevsky's manuscript. The work so fired their imaginations that they spent a whole night reading it and rushed to Dostoevsky early in the morning to congratulate him. Later that day Nekrasov took the manuscript to Belinsky with the claim that he had found a new Gogol. 'With you, new Gogols grow like mushrooms,' was the critic's tart response. He agreed to read *Poor Folk* and immediately ordered that the unknown young author be brought to him, an event which Dostoevsky described 30 years later with the requisite awe:

Belinsky *began a fiery speech, his eyes blazing.*

'Have you yourself any idea,' he said over and over in a high-pitched voice, 'what you've written here?' His voice used to become high-pitched whenever he spoke with strong feeling. 'It's only through your direct awareness as a writer that you've been able to write like this, but have you really understood the terrible truth you've revealed to us? It can't be that at 20 or so you've been able to understand it all.'[13]

Praise from such an authority as Belinsky became *a moment of triumph in my life,* as Dostoevsky put it, *I had made a breakthrough, something completely new had begun but something I had never imagined in my wildest dreams. (I was a great dreamer at that time.)*[14] He had achieved virtual overnight renown.

What exactly was the 'terrible truth' Belinsky thought Dostoevsky had revealed?

Poor Folk is a short novel based on an exchange of letters between an elderly impoverished civil servant, Makar Devushkin, and a girl, Varenka Dobroselova, upon whom he dotes, which was a somewhat dated literary form even for the 1840s. It is important as a variety of confessional literature in which the squalor of urban poverty, pungently described though it is, forms a backdrop to Devushkin's discovery of personality, lending his portrayal a much more psychologically perceptive and sympathetic edge than can be claimed for Gogol's portrayal of the type of the 'poor clerk'. In fact, the protagonists are not really 'poor folk'; they do not demonstrate the 'insolence' of poverty, as Devushkin defines it. The sentimentalism of Varenka's portrait militates against this and a certain marked 'literariness' of style and reference give the work a contrived and parodic air, but the contrivance involved in portraying Devushkin shows above all Dostoevsky's powers of literary impersonation, his voicing of character, so that at the end, when Varenka leaves him to get married to the villain of the piece, his final letter displays a fragmentation of personality that suggests total breakdown and the onset of a human tragedy far greater than the loss of an overcoat.

Poor Folk may hardly move us nowadays, but Belinsky saw in it the 'terrible truth' of social humiliation and injustice, features endemic to Russian society; Dostoevsky manifestly intended it as a Balzacian study in personality types and relationships with a marked emotional and psychological bias. It is hardly surprising, therefore, that his second original work would explore the issue of breakdown of personality in his study of Goliadkin, at the mercy of persecution mania, whose problem becomes pathological in the shape of Goliadkin junior, his double and persecutor.

The Double (*Dvoinik*, 1846) was even further removed from Belinsky's social criteria for inclusion in the 'natural school' of literature, though he approved the power of the writing, but it shed light on Dostoevsky's preoccupation with the Gothic, the realm of dreams and self-delusion. A distinctive part of this new approach was the compression of all the events in the story of Goliadkin's breakdown into four days and the use of a particular, near-theatrical type of set scene, known as the *skandal* scene, in which the central figure is subjected to a cumulative and deeply traumatic form of social humiliation. These two features, first evident in *The Double*, if adumbrated in the earlier work, were to become hallmarks of Dostoevsky's manner in his major fiction.

No less marked was his genuflecting to the Gogolian habit of near-burlesque treatment of narrative with an artful humour, rendered here blacker and all the more ironic through the impersonating role of the malicious double and the contrivance of supposing that it was all a detailed case history.

Once fame came to him, the young Dostoevsky's shyness and sense of class inferiority proved serious handicaps. He was fêted in St Petersburg literary society even before his work was published. The praise went to his head, as his letters to his brother reveal, and the sudden access of arrogant self-confidence quickly aroused resentment. Introduced to the society of the Panaevs, he appeared gauche, made tentative overtures to his hostess, Madame Panaeva, who evidently regarded him as immature, and soon found himself the butt of jokes.

Ivan Turgenev

It was a period when other young men of his generation were entering the literary scene, among whom the most prominent and gifted was Ivan Turgenev (1818–83). After initially being friends, a rivalry quickly developed and Turgenev became one of the hyper-sensitive Dostoevsky's wickedest tormentors through the circulation of some doggerel in which the latter was described, among other things, as 'a red pimple on the nose of literature'. The distress of this and other forms of finger-pointing rankled with Dostoevsky for the rest of his life.

Quarrelling, however, with those whom he considered his rivals or those who attempted to exert their authority over him merely mirrored the enmities and highly emotional states he depicted in his fiction. Allied to this were intellectual conflicts with clear political implications that provoked intense debate among the

Wilhelm Hegel

Friedrich W J Schelling (1775–1854) was most influential in Russia in terms of aesthetic theory. Georg Wilhelm Friedrich Hegel (1770–1831) was largely interpreted as the proponent of 'reconciliation with reality' although his philosophical legacy produced a Left– Hegelian ideology of action and materialism represented by Ludwig Andreas Feuerbach (1804–72) who attacked religious belief and argued that Man should be substituted for God as the real object of veneration. Max Stirner (1806–56) proclaimed the importance of the autonomous ego and the liberating power of free will.

first generation of the Russian intelligentsia, the so-called 'men of the 40s'. A rich brew of new ideas had begun to replace the Romanticism and German idealistic philosophy of the previous decade. Instead of Schelling and Hegel among the German influences there were Feuerbach and Stirner, but more important than these were the influences emanating from France under the general banner of utopian socialism. Belinsky was the first leading Russian authority to proclaim a commitment to socialism and it was he who tried to influence Dostoevsky in the direction of socialist beliefs.

The precise extent of Belinsky's influence is hard to judge. A leading Russian commentator has argued that 'throughout almost all his literary work Dostoevsky struggled with Belinsky, as in the biblical story Jacob struggled with the Lord.'[15] Dostoevsky, who had been so impressed as a child by the sufferings of Job, felt an affinity with Belinsky, who was of a similar social background and suffered increasingly from the affliction of tuberculosis. Mention of Christ brought tears to Dostoevsky's eyes, Belinsky apparently claimed, but Belinsky's notion that Christ, if he were to return to earth, would become a socialist and follow Feuerbach sounded like blasphemy to Dostoevsky and revealed what seemed like atheism at the heart of the critic's utopian socialism. This was undoubtedly unfair to Belinsky, whose enthusiasm could be misdirected but always retained a Christian purpose, even if humanistic. Somewhat inevitably a rift occurred between them (probably in 1846), due as much perhaps to issues of loyalty as of ideology. Belinsky had finally escaped Kraevsky's clutches and become in 1847 the moving spirit of a newly revived journal, *The Contemporary* (*Sovremennik*). He sought contributors, but Dostoevsky was already in thrall to Kraevsky and financial need dictated his adherence. Ideologically, Dostoevsky never forgot the critic who had first recognized his talent. The greatest testimony to this was his final and most memorable creation, Ivan Karamazov, who, echoing Belinsky, cannot accept the justice of God's world and wants to return his entrance ticket.

If Dostoevsky found himself alienated from the literary circles of St Petersburg, others proved more accessible. A former classmate of his at the Academy, Aleksei Beketov, had formed a group that devoted itself to discussing socialist questions and even made a tentative effort to put socialism into effect by forming a commune. Among the participants in the circle were the brothers Maikov, of whom Valerian Maikov became a close intimate. He praised Dostoevsky's work when others began to belittle it, defended the writer's freedom to write as he wished and displayed a sympathetic understanding of his literary approach, Valerian's tragic death in 1847 caused a loss of support that may have contributed to an awakening of Dostoevsky's interest in more radical methods than those advocated by an idealistic utopianism.

Less easy to assess is the extent to which illness and indebtedness affected his relationships. The evidence for Dostoevsky's

Mikhail Petrashevsky

epilepsy at this period is uncertain, but if one accepts the testimony of his friend, Dr Yanovsky, it seems likely that one or two episodes occurred which might be interpreted as epileptic, even if they were not fully symptomatic of the falling sickness. According to the doctor's testimony and even Dostoevsky's own claims,[16] he was affected by some form of malaise towards the end of the 1840s. He refers to it as hypochondria, even a kind of madness that manifested itself in a highly nervous and depressed condition. Reflected though this was in his writing, it may also account for the unusual extent to which he became involved in what for him were dangerously subversive activities.

Acquaintanceship with Mikhail Butashevich-Petrashevsky and his circle was the beginning of Dostoevsky's conversion to revolutionary politics. The group in question was not in fact given to discussion of revolutionary issues. It was more of a talking shop or small forum, with hardly more than 20 participants at most meetings, devoted to orations, readings and disputes over 'liberal' matters. Awareness of such authorities as Fourier, Blanc and Proudhon, among others, was fashionable and their ideas were hotly debated.

Dostoevsky's contributions seem to have been confined to literary readings. He was never close to Petrashevsky and may well have attended the meetings at the latter's lodgings to enjoy the chance of a meal and some wine of notoriously poor quality. Being compassionate and humanitarian, he was naturally indignant at the violent subjection of the serfs and is known to have protested at the brutal punishment of a peasant soldier. However, specific revolutionary utterances by him are largely based on hearsay. In one respect, though, he found a commitment and this was due to the influence of a member of the Petrashevsky circle whom Dostoevsky was said to have regarded as his Mephistopheles. Nikolai Speshnev had wealth, a strong personality and an ambition to do more than talk.[17] He lent Dostoevsky money, suborned him, it seems, by his charismatic charm, introduced him to active plotting against the Tsar, perhaps affected his health through the subsequent indebtedness and ultimately provided the model for Stavrogin, the sole image of a revolutionary leader in Dostoevsky's major fiction.

The plotting of revolution in any real sense was confined to a breakaway section of the Petrashevsky circle known as the Palm-Durov circle, which had formed in late 1848. Consisting at most of eight people, it was here that tentative plans were drawn up to write, print and distribute subversive, anti-Tsarist propaganda. Dostoevsky was known to have attempted to recruit the late Valerian Maikov's brother to this circle. Dostoevsky himself achieved notoriety for reading aloud a private letter that Belinsky had written to Gogol in response to the latter's highly sententious, sanctimonious and reactionary work, *Selected Passages*

Charles Fourier (1772–1837) was a somewhat dotty French 'utopian' thinker who became famous for the advocacy of 'phalansteries', that is, units of approximately 1,500 people living on communal lines. Louis Blanc (1811–82) argued pre-1848 that personal interests should be subservient to the welfare of the community. Pierre-Joseph Proudhon (1809–65), famous for the notion that 'property is theft', was one of the greatest exponents of libertarian socialism.

from a Correspondence with Friends (1847). Belinsky's *Letter to Gogol* was a masterly denunciation of Gogol's betrayal of the tenets of social justice that Belinsky held so dear. He demanded the abolition of serfdom and corporal punishment, argued for the rule of law, condemned the role of the Orthodox Church in Russian life, upheld Voltairean values and proclaimed that writers were the public's only true leaders, defenders and saviours from the autocracy. It was regarded as Belinsky's final testament and a work so subversive it could only be circulated in secret.

Early in 1848 revolution broke out in Paris. The regime in Russia was so shaken that it began to pay close attention to the activities of these hitherto relatively innocuous St Petersburg circles. In any case, revolution abroad naturally inflamed the seditious feelings that had led to the formation of the Palm-Durov circle and Speshnev's tentative plans for rebellion. A government spy was smuggled into the Petrashevsky circle and began assiduously reporting back on the subjects discussed and the identities of those attending. By the spring of 1849 Dostoevsky's name came to the attention of the authorities for having read aloud Belinsky's famous *Letter to Gogol* at one of the plenary meetings.

Nowhere in Dostoevsky's published writings or correspondence of this period can one find any overt mention of his support for revolution. Indeed, his literary work plumbed issues more related to pathology than politics, though rebellion against authority or, more specifically, against urban reality – a romantic, often unbalanced, challenge to the real – might be deemed to imply political dissidence of a sort (as it most certainly did in the Soviet Union). He published a series of short prose works exploring such issues as a dreamer's obsessive preoccupation with escaping reality (in the lyrical 'White Nights') or the power of romantic delirium (in 'The Landlady') that involved an eclectic mix of folk legend and hints of incest. As for the contrast between the self-delusion of the isolated individual and a utopian communalism touched on in

The Exchange and the Peter and Paul Fortress from the River Neva, St Petersburg

'Mr Prokharchin', with its much more obvious analysis of miserliness and capitalism, it may obliquely reflect issues raised in the Petrashevsky circle; it is doubtful whether 'A Weak Heart', an odd little study of a poor clerk driven mad by happiness, should be overburdened with interpretation. In all his work of this period the main protagonists are solitary individuals, usually poor, seeking identity, personal dignity and a sense of belonging in an alien environment and compensating for their estrangement by resorting to dreams. Whether or not such a style of portraiture, such voicing of character, can be construed as uniquely Dostoevskian in its use of polyphony and by that token superior to the approach of other writers, as Bakhtin has implied, is questionable.[18]

None of Dostoevsky's creations of the late 1840s matches the depth and interest of Devushkin in *Poor Folk* and all are marked by degrees of emotional immaturity. Even his attempt at a novel, *Netochka Nezvanova* (1849), published anonymously after his arrest, is an episodic work devoted to exploring the heroine's adolescent infatuations for her deluded stepfather and then for the daughter of her benefactor, the young Princess Katia. Although Netochka provides some sort of narrative thread, the unfinished novel appears to illustrate Dostoevsky's view of the genre as being packed with events and characters on a Dickensian scale. In all his work of this period, however, he demonstrated a remarkable articulacy, a free-flowing, idiomatic, often sardonic manner, and rare powers of observation both in evoking the urban scene and in characterization through naturalistic dialogue.

In the early morning of 23 April 1849 Dostoevsky was arrested and taken to the notorious Peter and Paul Fortress where he was placed in cell No. 9 of the Alekseevsky Ravelin. With little access to daylight, in conditions of damp, foul air and poor food, he was to endure months of solitary imprisonment during which his health deteriorated and he became increasingly subject to nightmares and bouts of insomnia. The onset of summer weather brought a slight improvement. He took the opportunity to write one of his most charming and sunny short works, 'A Little Hero', set in a provincial rather than an urban world and recounting how a young boy retrieves a lost love letter and successfully returns it to the heroine. His love for her made him experience *my first conscious awareness of my heart, the first but as yet unclear insight into my own nature . . . My first childhood ended at that instant.*[19] This moment of insight is the first instance of incipient maturity in any of Dostoevsky's heroes of the 1840s and for Dostoevsky himself it may have represented a fundamental renunciation of all his recent concerns.

In the course of the ensuing investigations he made no attempt to deny his participation in the Petrashevsky meetings, or his professed 'liberalism', or his association with the Palm-Durov circle. He was not disloyal to any of his co-conspirators. The only charges finally brought against him concerned his reading of the subversive *Letter to Gogol* and his presence during the reading of another supposedly dissident work. By no standard of civilized justice could such charges merit execution by firing squad, but it was to this punishment that he was sentenced.

On the morning of 22 December 1849 Dostoevsky and 20 others were driven from the Peter and Paul Fortress to Semenovksy Square where a scaffold had been erected. The prisoners were assembled in two rows on the scaffold facing the troops and their sentences were read out. A priest offered the condemned men a last chance to kiss the cross before the first three were hooded and taken off the scaffold to be tied to stakes. Petrashevsky, ever the exhibitionist, though not without courage, tore off his hood while at the stake. The gesture was in vain. Within moments of the firing squad being ordered to take aim a

The execution of Petrashevsky, Semenovsky Square 22 December 1849

carriage entered the square bringing news that Tsar Nicholas I had commuted the death sentence to one of penal servitude.

Dostoevsky had awaited execution in the second row after Petrashevsky. His brush with death reverberated through the rest of his life. Shackled though he was and in chains, he returned to his cell full of joy at having been given back his life. He had little to celebrate in fact, for he had been sentenced to four years of penal servitude followed by service in the ranks, but writing to his brother on 22 December 1849 he displayed great forbearance and courage. His career had been ruined; lesser men might have been crushed. Instead Dostoevsky appeared reborn out of the disaster:

As I look back on the past I think how much time I have wasted, how much of it has been lost in errors, in mistakes, in idleness, in an inability to live properly; how little I treasured it and how often I sinned against my heart and my spirit – and my heart is overwhelmed. Life is a gift, life is happiness, every minute can be a lifetime of happiness. Si jeunesse savait! ['If youth only knew!'] *Now, in changing my life I am being reborn in a new form. Dear brother, I swear to you I will not lose hope and I will keep my spirit and my heart pure! I will be born again for the better. That is my sole hope, my sole comfort.*[20]

Early in 1850 Dostoevsky left European Russia for Siberia. He would not return for ten years.

Siberia and Silence

Incarcerated in the penal settlement of Omsk for four years, Dostoevsky was cut off from European Russia and any communication with his brother, let alone new ideas and new literary developments. He was plunged into the midst of peasant convicts who despised his educated status, resented his social apartness as an ex-nobleman stripped of his rights and had little in common with him save the terrible irony that his literary preoccupation with lives lived in cramped urban confinement was now transfigured into a more terrible reality of barracks, prison shackles, hard labour, sickness, squalor, violence, total absence of personal freedom and little human dignity beyond the right to dream.

Exile to Siberia, an English wood engraving of 1874

His sole reading matter was a copy of the New Testament donated to him by Natalia Fonvizina, a wife of one of the Decembrists sentenced to Siberian exile after December 1825.[21] Dostoevsky was incarcerated in what he called 'the house of the dead' (literally 'the dead house'), as he described it in *Memoirs from the House of the Dead* (*Zapiski iz mertvogo doma*, 1860–62), his published record of the four years spent in that hell. For censorship reasons, if for no other, this account (offered as the notes of a wife-murderer) probably modified and glossed over the more terrible aspects. Apart from constant weak health, it is possible Dostoevsky may have suffered a flogging and developed epilepsy as a consequence, though this is uncertain; the testimony for those four years must of course remain his own, however partial. What one may say without fear of contradiction is that, as a masterpiece of prison literature, it cannot be read even today without a shudder.

He made no close friends, it seems, among the peasant convicts. He was appalled and fascinated by the evidence of evil he encountered in the criminals with whom he daily brushed shoulders. The lack of remorse exhibited by the worst of them for unspeakable crimes against children and women – not to mention the mass murderer, Orlov, who was steely and self-controlled beyond belief – directed Dostoevsky's thoughts inevitably to crime and its psychological meaning. In all of his future major fiction he made murder the focus of his attention and criminality a central issue. No vision of the degradation to which human beings can subject themselves was more awful than the squalidly detailed picture he gave of a visit to the bathhouse:

When we flung open the door to the bathroom itself, I thought we had entered hell. Imagine a room twelve paces by twelve in which up to 100 men perhaps, certainly not less than 80, were all packed tight because the prisoners were divided into two shifts and there were 200 of us in all. Steam blinded one's eyes, there was such filth and dirt and it was so crowded one didn't know where to step [. . .] Steam increased by the moment. It was not just hot, it was scorching. Everyone shouted and screamed to the sound of a hundred chains scraping across the floor . . . Some men in trying to move became entangled in the chains of others and then got mixed up with the heads of those below them, fell down, swore and pulled others down with them. Filth poured from all sides. All were in a kind of drunken, frenzied state and everywhere yells and shouts resounded [. . .] Prisoners' shaven heads and heat-reddened bodies seemed uglier than ever. On steamy, sweaty spines the welts from whippings and beatings stood out clearly, so that now they looked newly raw. Frightful welts! A chill ran down my back at the sight of them. Then it became steamier still and the whole room was filled with a thick, burning-hot cloud and everyone started screaming and yelling again.[22]

Though Dostoevsky was treated more harshly than other former members of the Petrashevsky circle, he always insisted later that among the most important things he learned from his years of incarceration was the need for unity among the different layers and sections of Russian society. A romantic and idealistic notion no doubt, prompted, it seems, chiefly by the shared and unifying experience of theatricals in the penal settlement. Along, of course, with the horrors were the small kindnesses, the moments when the peasant convicts showed him compassion, although only two of his fellow unfortunates (the prisoners were known as 'unfortunates') left happy memories with him, the Lezgin Nurra and Alei, the Dagestan Tatar, neither of whom was Russian. Money was always needed to purchase favours and alleviate the worst circumstances. Ultimately Dostoevsky survived with two paramount needs. The first was the need for privacy or as he put it in his letter to Fonvizina after being released in 1854: *The society of human beings can become a poison and plague and it is precisely from this insufferable torment that I have had to endure most in these four years.*[23] The second was the need for Christ. In the same letter he made the following famous confession of faith:

I will tell you about myself that I am a child of the age, a child of disbelief and doubt up to this time and even (I know this) to the moment they put the lid on my coffin. Such awful torments I have suffered and I still suffer now from this thirst for faith, which is always the stronger in my soul the greater are my arguments against it. And yet God sometimes sends me moments when I am completely at peace; at those times I love, and I find that I am loved by others, and in such moments I have composed for myself a symbol of faith, in which everything for me is lucid and holy. This symbol is very simple, it is: to believe there is nothing more beautiful, profound, loving, wise, courageous and perfect than Christ, and not only is there not, but I tell myself with jealous love that there cannot be. What is more, if someone proved to me that Christ was outside the truth, and it was really true *that the truth was outside Christ, then I would still prefer to remain with Christ than with the truth.*[24]

The very contentiousness expressed here, with its stubborn insistence on commitment to Christ regardless of truth, was what sustained Dostoevsky throughout the martyrdom of penal servitude. From this lowest point in his life he would slowly make a gradual ascent towards recognition and fame as a writer of world stature. But the path would never be easy, the torments always awful; and the first of such torments was lack of freedom.

When finally released from the penal settlement at Omsk, he was sent to barracks in Semipalatinsk to serve as a common soldier. At least he was now able to write to his brother asking for funds and a curious assortment of reading matter including the Koran, works by the German philosophers Immanuel Kant (1724–1804) and G W F Hegel (1770–1831) and French translations of classical works by the Greek historian Herodotus (*c*.484–*c*.420 BC) and the Greek philosopher Plutarch (*c*.50–*c*.120). Dostoevsky gradually renewed contact with members of his immediate family and through personal contacts and some financial help he was able to escape from the barracks and rent a room in the Russian quarter of Semipalatinsk. A major change occurred when he became friendly with Baron Wrangel, an intelligent young admirer who had been newly appointed as public prosecutor. Their friendship would be close and long-lasting. Dostoevsky now had the chance to seriously discuss all manner of new issues during what was to become a period of great change for Russia after the Crimean War, but in essence he remained gagged and imprisoned as a writer through not being allowed to publish.

The first wife, Maria Isaeva

Denied female company for so long, it is hardly surprising that he fell in love or that his choice should have been so mistaken. Maria Isaeva (familiarly known as Marsha) was unhappily married to a drunken officer. She took pity on Dostoevsky as a man with no future (or so Wrangel reports in his memoirs)[25] and he possibly mistook such sympathy for reciprocated passion. The Isaevs were generally considered too louche for the snobbish upper crust of provincial society, which no doubt attracted Dostoevsky to them. Marsha had some claims to distinction in that her father was a school director and her grandfather a Frenchman who had fled during the Revolution, but she herself was sickly, intense, fickle and inclined to hysteria – the very model, in fact, of several of Dostoevsky's heroines.

The courtship advanced with great difficulty. They were separated through the appointment of Marsha's husband to a lowly post in Kuznetsk some 600 kilometres away; in any case,

Dostoevsky in Semipalatinsk 1858

Dostoevsky had little status of his own – all he could offer her were floods of letters, of which only one has survived. It was not until October 1856, after Dostoevsky had written to Totleben – famous for his fortification of Sevastopol during the Crimean War and known to him through the Academy of Engineers – that the Tsar gave permission for his promotion to officer status. In the meantime Marsha had been widowed. She finally consented to remarry and in February 1857 Dostoevsky and his new bride sanctified their union in Kuznetsk before returning to Semipalatinsk. During the journey another and more incapacitating form of imprisonment became apparent when, to Marsha's horror, Dostoevsky suffered a serious epileptic seizure. In the early months of their marriage his epilepsy became more marked, the attacks more frequent, so that there were now good medical reasons for his discharge from military service. Although by April 1857 Dostoevsky's nobility status had been restored, he did not receive his final discharge from the army until December 1858, but by this time his literary career had showed the first signs of tentative renewal.

It had begun in April 1857 with the anonymous publication in

Kraevsky's *Fatherland Notes* of 'A Little Hero', a short story he had written while in the Peter and Paul Fortress. Life in Semipalatinsk had meanwhile supplied him with ample material for new work. 'Uncle's Dream' ('Diadushkin son', 1859) and 'The Village of Stepanchikovo' ('Selo Stepanchikovo', 1859), the two works he composed in Siberian exile, are comic studies of provincial society that owe something to Gogol, while demonstrating their Dostoevskian uniqueness through elements of farce. Neither is especially memorable, though both have value as pointers to his later development.

'Uncle's Dream' probably had theatrical origins. It is almost a short novel, packed with dialogue and examples of the *skandal* scene condensed into what is supposedly a 24-hour time-span. It concerns an elderly symbol of hereditary authority, a comic prince, an artificial creation literally stuck together, who is sought after by a provincial *dame de salon* as a match for her daughter. The resulting comic analysis of provincial Russian society at its sickest is noteworthy chiefly for the way in which Dostoevsky's emphasis has clearly shifted from concentration on the solitary individual (so conspicuous in his studies of urban life) to an awareness of a new 'psychology' characteristic of the provinces. This 'psychology' is defined principally by its lack of privacy:

Every provincial lives, as it were, under a bell-glass. There is not the slightest likelihood of his being able to hide anything from his respected co-provincials. They know one by heart and even know what one doesn't even know about oneself. A provincial must by his very nature, it seems, be a psychologist and one well versed in the ways of the heart.[26]

However tongue in cheek such a definition may be, the absence of privacy in the prison barracks, as in the gossipy world of Semipalatinsk, must have contributed to this new emphasis on multiple characters and themes, on groups of characters, their mutual inquisitiveness and interrelatedness, in ways that virtually exclude their solitary side. The bases of Dostoevsky's major fiction, structurally speaking, are to be found here and if 'Uncle's Dream' is of only marginal interest, 'The Village of Stepanchikovo' anticipates quite clearly the form of Dostoevsky's mature novels.

In aspects of its setting, characterization and structure it points forward to *The Brothers Karamazov.* Static and analytical, it introduces a feature Dostoevsky had not used so conspicuously before on such a scale: a narrator. In this case he is an eager, inoffensive and amiable narrator, but clearly uncertain of his role and irrelevant, by and large, to the ideological conflict at the heart of his narrative. This conflict – expressed through the lectures to which a loquacious buffoon, Foma Opiskin, subjects his good-natured host – involves the ridicule of Dostoevsky's principal literary mentor, Gogol, and parodies the older author's sententious *Selected Passages from Correspondence with Friends* (1847). It also involves an attack on all forms of authority, on the supposed power wielded by one person over another and the human weakness for believing in great men – in short, it raises the whole issue of discipleship and possession by ideas in a way that demonstrates how, for Dostoevsky, ideological issues have begun to match and supersede emotional ones. If his major novels have the distinction of being ideological and complex in their interrelated sub-plots, then they have their beginnings in 'The Village of Stepanchikovo' and its ludicrous inhabitants.

In July 1859 Dostoevsky, his wife and stepson, Pasha (who was to prove particularly irksome to him later) left Siberia for good. Almost a decade earlier, he had crossed the Urals in chains and had nearly frozen to death, but now he went by sledge and in warm weather. He raised a glass of orange liqueur in farewell to Asia and enjoyed wild strawberries in anticipation of arrival in Europe. That he looked forward to great happiness as well is less likely. Marriage had not brought him love and scarcely seems to have involved true companionship. It had involved costs that Dostoevsky naturally hoped to defray with his writing, but ini-

The drawing room of the Dostoevsky house in St Petersburg

tially he was not allowed to return to the centre of literary activity in St Petersburg and had to content himself with several months' stay in provincial Tver. Meanwhile, he had changed fundamentally from the young man who had toyed with revolutionary ideas. He returned to European Russia a convinced patriot, belligerent in his conviction of Russia's spiritual superiority over the West, only to confront a state of intense ideological debate in which radical concerns had become predominant.

The most significant change was the marked difference between the generations of the intelligentsia. Socially speaking, the intelligentsia that had existed when Dostoevsky was condemned to penal servitude in the 1840s had been composed of a disaffected nobility with largely liberal leanings. The chief literary representative of 'the Men of the 40s' was Ivan Turgenev (1818–83). Initially famous for his depiction of the rural world of landowners and peasants in his *Sketches from a Hunter's Album* (*Zapiski okhotnika*, 1852), he later became the chronicler of the generation of 'superfluous men' in his novels *Rudin* (1856) and *Home of the*

Gentry (*Dvorianskoe gnezdo*, 1859). By the time Dostoevsky returned to St Petersburg in December 1859 Turgenev was recognized as the leading Russian writer of the age, whose sensitive and lyrical evocations of a rural world in which the intelligentsia hero's love is challenged by a strong-minded heroine had established a literary model for the future.

Political message had become second nature to literary purpose. The finest example of this was the publication of Ivan Goncharov's masterpiece *Oblomov* (1859), a monumental study of an apathetic nobleman that gave rise to a brilliant piece of criticism by the *enfant terrible* Nikolai Dobroliubov (1836–61) entitled *What is Oblomovism?* (*Chto takoe Oblomovshchina?* 1859). Dobroliubov pointed to the political – or socio-political – implication of the dressing-gown existence of Oblomov by suggesting that his apathy was directly attributable to the serf-owning ethos from which he derived. What Russian society now needed was a younger, active, radical generation composed of *raznochintsy*,[27] of non-nobility origin, that is to say, from the priesthood (Dobroliubov himself was of that background) or the medical professions and government service.

In the half-dozen years immediately succeeding the defeat of imperial Russia in the Crimean War these younger members of the Russian intelligentsia became known as 'the New Men' or 'the Sons' and their leading spokesmen were Dobroliubov himself and Nikolai Chernyshevsky (1828–89), his senior partner on the leading radical journal *The Contemporary*. Their programme in the run-up to the emancipation of the serfs in 1861 was implicitly more radical than the gradualist, liberal programme for change advocated by the older generation of 'the Fathers' to whom Turgenev belonged. Nevertheless it was Turgenev who first attempted to delineate the aspirations of 'the Sons' in literary terms. His novel *On the Eve* (*Nakanune*, 1860) indicated by its very title the likelihood of change on the eve of the forthcoming liberation of the serfs, although its hero (a somewhat wooden representation of a revolutionary) is less striking as an agent of change than the heroine, Elena, who repudiates her background and past in order to sacrifice herself in the cause of liberating the hero's native Bulgaria.

More important in relation to the literature of the period was the search for a positive hero. Dobroliubov, among others, clamoured for the creation of such a type, but the programmatic literature required for such a representation ran counter to the freedoms sought by its most gifted practitioners. On the one side in this conflict of interests there was Turgenev, who attempted to diagnose the issue of types in his fascinating study of Don Quixote as an altruistic extrovert and Hamlet as an egotistical introvert.[28] On the other side, Chernyshevsky argued for an art that had to be secondary to reality and therefore socially useful in its purpose (see his Feuerbachian treatment of aesthetics in 'The Aesthetic Relations of Art to Reality', 1855); to which he added his materialistic treatment of what he called the 'anthropological principle in philosophy' (1860), which argued against the spiritual side of humanity and denied the notion of free will in favour of a utilitarian 'rational egoism'.

It was into this cloud of ideas that Dostoevsky found himself catapulted on his return to St Petersburg.[29] Greeted as he was by his beloved brother Mikhail – who had already achieved permission to publish a new journal called *Time* (*Vremia*) – Dostoevsky returned armed with his own convictions as well the aura of martyrdom bestowed on him by his experiences. At the forefront of his convictions, of course, was a paramount belief in freedom. One of his earliest pieces of journalism was an attack on Dobroliubov's advocacy of a socially committed literature and a vigorous defence of literary freedom (by implication, freedom from censorship). But equally important for him was the role he now sought to adopt in the polemical atmosphere of the times *vis-à-vis* the peasantry.

Both wings of the intelligentsia – 'the Fathers' and 'the Sons' – had become preoccupied by the need for change in their attitude to the peasantry, but Dostoevsky's stance, once he had a forum for his ideas in *Time*, was essentially different from either wing. He advocated a 'philosophy of the soil' (known as *pochvennost'* or *pochvennichestvo*, from *pochva*: 'soil'). It ruled out class conflict in favour of Christian and especially peasant virtues of humility and reconciliation from which the educated and privileged classes should learn. Such an idealistic vision of harmony, although broadly Slavophile[30] in its origin and appeal, became for Dostoevsky emblematic of the reconciling role that he wished for Russia in its relations with Europe and implicit in the later evolution of this idea into the Messianism of a Russian Christ.

Slavophilism evolved as a body of ideas in the 1840s as a reaction to the increasing advocacy of Western influences – Vissarion Belinsky (1811–48) was a leading proponent of such influences. The Slavophiles insisted on a return to what they conceived of as a pre-Petrine social utopianism based on the teachings of Orthodoxy and an idealized peasant commune. Profoundly conservative, even politically reactionary, their ideas achieved wide appeal in Russia after the Crimean War and Dostoevsky was not alone in being influenced by them.[x]

From *Time* to the Underground

Dostoevsky invested all of his hopes for his literary future in *Time*, the new journal established with the help of his brother Mikhail. Although *Time* attracted such contributors as the playwright Alexander Ostrovsky (1823–86), the poet Nikolai Nekrasov (1821–77) and the satirist Mikhail Saltykov (1826–89), Dostoevsky's own work – *Memoirs from the House of the Dead* and his next novel *The Insulted and Injured* (*Unizhennye i oskorblennye,* 1861) – helped to ensure the journal's popularity and soon gained it as many as 4,000 subscribers.

In the turbulent disputes of the period *Time*'s ideological position was not as radical as *The Contemporary*'s, nor was it markedly reactionary. Relatively middle-of-the-road in its advocacy of the idealistic 'philosophy of the soil', its readership may have been unclear as to the journal's real political orientation; and yet, the fact that its editor was an ex-convict made the authorities suspicious. *Time* published, for example, a translation of *Mary Barton* (1848) by Elizabeth Gaskell (1810–65), a daring exposé of the plight of the working class in Manchester. More subversive, perhaps, in the light of the clamour for realism in literature, was Dostoevsky's insistence that the 'real' should embrace the fantastic as

Dostoevsky in 1863

well as the supposedly factual; and, in any case, the value of all literature must depend on the ability to write well and the human need for beauty.

His feuilleton contributions, as well as his so-called feuilleton-novel *The Injured and Insulted*, demonstrated this approach, enhanced by an expressive and remarkably fluent style. The novel may have owed a great deal to his admiration for Charles Dickens (1812–70) – including tear-jerking chapters devoted to a Nelly obviously drawn from Little Nell in *The Old Curiosity Shop* (1841) – but it also contained several uniquely Dostoevskian features. Set in St Petersburg, it is narrated by a beginning writer who resembles Dostoevsky in the 1840s, but grafted on to this nostalgic quality, with its accompanying sentimentalism, is the present time of the fiction and the sad tale of the narrator's love for Natasha (the daughter of a provincial family engaged in litigation against the wicked Prince Valkovsky), her love for the prince's spineless son and the narrator's concern for the 12-year-old Nelly caught in the meshes of the prince's wickedness and the surrounding urban squalor. Basically melodramatic as a tale, the novel deserves our attention for the way it emphasizes the confrontation between the provincial and urban worlds, the psychological differences characteristic of them and the horror pervading the labyrinthine recesses of the city.

The narrator experiences this horror as something 'mystical': *It is the most oppressive, tormenting fear which I can't define, of something incomprehensible and non-existent in the order of things but something that will happen immediately, perhaps this very second and, as if in mockery of everything rational, will come and stand before me as an undeniable fact, horrific, ugly and inexorable.*[31] It is a sense of horror at the power of the city to alienate human beings (akin to the horror that may afflict those who are frightened of corpses), but it is associated here with Nelly's arrival in the fiction and all the horrific aspects of her 'underground' world. The emphasis placed on the suddenness of the fear is a feature common to Dostoevsky's manner in this novel as in so many later ones, for, despite its often long-winded dialogue exchanges, it is characterized by swift changes of tone, from farce to Grand Guignol, from love to terror. Reminiscent of *The Double* as a study of alienation and persecution, more central to the novel, psychologically, is the contrast between the persecuted characters of *the insulted and injured* and the source of such persecution in the evil epitomized by Prince Valkovsky.

Two types of egoism are at play in this contrast. On the one hand an 'egoism of suffering', a masochistic delight in being persecuted, is essential to the portrayal of Nelly who, as the narrator defines her, *literally took pleasure in her pain, this 'egoism of suffering', if I can call it that. This aggravating of her pain and her enjoyment of it were understandable to me; it was the pleasure experienced by many insulted and injured persecuted by fate and aware of its injustice.*[32] On the other hand, the evil inherent in Valkovsky's egoism is far more sophisticated. Overwrought and dangerously close to melodramatic villainy, he is portrayed as having a personality supposedly dominated by evil. His duplicity is particularly evident in the ambivalence of his eyes, which epitomize, in their alternation of seeming honesty and manifest depravity, the sinister power that the urban world could exert over the narrator and most of the characters. Valkovsky's frank confession of his sensuality and self-abasement in lust challenges and undercuts the high-minded utopianism of the younger generation. As the first real advocate of uninhibited free will to be found in Dostoevsky's works, Prince

> *Your attention would be particularly drawn by* [Valkovsky's] *apparently beautiful eyes, grey and frank. They alone, as it were, were unable to submit completely to his will. He might want them to have a soft and tender look, but the rays of his eyes seemed to alternate and between the soft, tender rays shone others that were mistrustful, querying, wicked.*
>
> The Injured and Insulted[33]

Valkovsky represents the grossest egotistical nihilism and a life lived cynically devoid of ideals.

Dostoevsky's view of human nature as only properly identifiable through such irrational and nihilistic impulses had a tragically ironic relevance to the spirit of the times. In the wake of the liberation of the serfs in February 1861, something resembling a revolutionary state of mind began to affect Russian society. No one diagnosed this situation better, in literary terms, than Turgenev in his novel *Fathers and Sons* (*Ottsy i deti*, 1862). In the figure of its hero, Bazarov, nihilism is portrayed as a denial of all accepted authorities save those justified by the natural sciences and a readiness to clear the ground for the future. That the portrait is also tragic – since Bazarov dies prematurely from typhoid after performing an autopsy – serves to heighten the impact of what was implied by nihilism. In a human sense, was Bazarov doomed by fate? In a political sense, was he a revolutionary (as Turgenev suggested in response to criticism of his masterpiece)? Or was his revolt in a moral sense an arrogant attempt on man's part to usurp the role of God? For Dostoevsky it seems likely that it was the latter and he seems to have been one of the very few to appreciate the significance of Turgenev's masterly interpretation of this new phenomenon in Russian life.

Fathers and Sons was attacked by *The Contemporary* as a slander on the younger generation and soon after its publication fires broke out in St Petersburg. They were thought to be the work of nihilists and arsonists. Worse still, Dostoevsky was shocked to find a leaflet entitled *Young Russia* on his doorstep. It proclaimed imminent revolution and the creation of a socialist state. So angered was he by such evident sedition that he paid a quick visit to Chernyshevsky to urge him to be less overtly radical in the orientation of *The Contemporary*. He was too late. The Government, panicked by peasant unrest as well as the recent disturbances, took measures to suppress further dissidence and arrested

Chernyshevsky in June 1862. At the same time Dostoevsky applied to go abroad. His reasons for such a trip were ostensibly medical, but he could now afford it and, in any case, it had been his ambition since boyhood to visit Western Europe.

No Russian visitor to Europe could be said to be more sceptical and nihilistic than Dostoevsky. In ironic justification of his own account of his travels in *Winter Notes of Summer Impressions* (*Zimnie zametki o letnikh vpechatleniakh*, 1863) he quoted the French saying that *Le Russe est sceptique et moqueur.*[34] One need hardly have been surprised, therefore, that Berlin looked like St Petersburg to him except that it was full of Germans or that the West, especially Paris, resembled a whited sepulchre where the overlay of culture and superiority merely concealed avarice and love of possessions. As for London, Dostoevsky's initial impression of its commercial vitality and sheer size left him overwhelmed. Second impressions left him aware of the grotesque extremes of wealth and poverty. If there was a metropolitan hell on earth, it was the Haymarket and the multitude of prostitutes who thronged there, including children offered for sale by their mothers. In the midst of them he encountered a small girl of no more than six years old, ragged, barefoot, dirty, hollow-cheeked, her body covered in bruises:

She wandered as if uncaring, not hurrying anywhere, drifting God knows why in the crowd; perhaps she was hungry. No one paid her any attention. But what astonished me most of all was the way she wandered with a look of such sadness, such inescapable desperation on her face, so that to see such a tiny creature bearing such a weight of abuse and hopelessness was even somehow unnatural, somehow terribly painful. She continually shook her dishevelled head from side to side as if debating something with herself, spread out her little hands and gesticulated, suddenly crossed them and pressed them to her bare chest. I turned and gave her a sixpence. She grabbed the silver coin, then wildly, with frightened astonishment, looked me in the eyes and suddenly ran away as fast as she could as if afraid I'd take the money back.[35]

Alexander Herzen (1812–70) chose to exile himself from Russia even before the Paris revolution of 1848 and later set up a Free Russian printing-press in London which published his journal *The Bell* (*Kolokol*, 1857–67). Smuggled into Russia, it was enormously influential prior to 1861 and the emancipation of the serfs in exposing official malpractices. Herzen had been a leading figure in the first generation of the intelligentsia during the 1840s and his memory is now best preserved in his famous memoirs *Past and Thoughts* (*Byloe i dumy*, 1852–5), a brilliant political chronicle of the principal events and figures in the development of the Russian intelligentsia.

This horrifying literary snapshot of a child's misery turned out to be more memorable to him than meeting the famous London exile, Alexander Herzen, whom every Russian visitor was expected to meet. Dostoevsky could not mention this meeting in print or by letter for fear of censorship, but it is not clear that Herzen was greatly impressed. They had in common a belief in the Russian peasantry, which for Herzen meant a somewhat idealistic assumption that the peasantry, uncontaminated by bourgeois aspirations and inherently democratic by virtue of the peasant commune, would become a nucleus of socialism; Dostoevsky never shared any such socio-political ideal. He may also have met Mikhail Bakunin, who had recently escaped from Siberia. In any case, Dostoevsky left London after only eight days and set off for Italy in the company of Strakhov, a leading contributor to *Time.* Their tour included Turin, Genoa and Florence where he found little to enjoy, it seemed, apart from a Raphael painting. No sooner had he entered the Uffizi than he ran out again. By early September he was back in St Petersburg.

Mikhail Bakunin (1814–76) had been, like Herzen, a leading figure among 'the Men of the 40s' but emigration to Europe led him eventually to become prominent as a theorist of anarchy and one of the founders of European anarchism.

In fact, three months of travel in Europe had left little lasting impact apart from his visit to

London's Crystal Palace on Sydenham Hill. This event was to stimulate the most profoundly polemical of his attacks on the socialist ideals of the younger generation. Meanwhile, after the arrest of Chernyshevsky, in July 1862 *The Contemporary* was closed for eight months and the position of *Time* became precarious. Dostoevsky published his account of his travels in *Time* between 1862 and 1863. Almost simultaneously, it seems, the imprisoned Chernyshevsky was composing his best-known work, the novel *What is to be Done?* (*Chto delat'?*, 1864). Through an extraordinary bungle by the censors, *The Contemporary* was permitted to publish it when it was up and running again in 1863 and *What is to be Done?* quickly achieved notoriety for its revolutionary assertion of female emancipation, free love, socialist working practices, the image of a new type of 'rigorist' hero and a vision of the future of humanity based on the Crystal Palace. To Dostoevsky these ideas, particularly the notion of rational egoism fundamental to them, were to prove a catalyst in defining his own deeply paradoxical interpretation of the human condition.

What is to be Done?, though banned shortly after publication, became enormously influential in clandestine form as a revolutionary text of Russian socialism. Among those influenced by Chernyshevsky's novel was Vladimir Ilich Lenin (1870–1924), who said that it 'fired my energies for a lifetime'.[36]

By early 1863, the Polish uprising against Russia had begun to concentrate minds. *Time* pursued a loyalist, pro-Russian line, but soon found itself outlawed after the publication of a needlessly sophisticated article by Strakhov on Russo–Polish relations. The closure of the journal in the summer of 1863 led to serious debts that affected Mikhail in particular, who had sold his cigarette factory to finance the publication. For Dostoevsky there were other complications. His epilepsy had worsened since his return from Europe and began to cause periods of severe depression. He felt he should go abroad in the hope of receiving treatment. Since there was no money available after the closure of the journal, he applied to the Literary Fund for an advance. He was an active member of the Fund, appearing in such activities as amateur theatricals and public readings on its behalf, and it may have been at one such occasion in 1861, when he read extracts from *The House of the Dead*, that a girl for whose sake he wished to make a second visit to Europe was in the audience.

Dostoevsky's marriage to Marsha had been clouded by her tuberculosis and their growing estrangement. In compensation he had found himself passionately infatuated by the young Polina (or Apollinaria) Suslova, who was approximately 20 years his junior and had been drawn to him initially, it seems, by his public readings and her own ambitions as an aspiring writer.[37] She became his mistress very possibly during the winter of 1862–3. Understandably coy and secretive about the relationship, Dostoevsky no doubt felt it could only be pursued satisfactorily in the relative anonymity of Paris. By August Polina was already waiting for him there and he set out to join her.

Apollinaria Suslova

En route he suddenly made a detour to Wiesbaden. Why he should have done this is unclear, though it could reasonably be supposed that he hoped to win enough in the casino to pay off his debts and cover the cost of the loan from the Literary Fund. So began a frenzied, love-hate relationship with the roulette wheel. The sheer excitement of challenging the capricious spin of the wheel in the belief that he could master it turned Dostoevsky's gambling into a mania and satisfied a deep-seated need to live recklessly, at the very limit of experience, much as he felt at moments of ecstasy during his epileptic seizures.

Possessed by this crazy euphoria, he finally reached Paris in mid-August 1863 only to have his worst fears confirmed: Polina had fallen for Salvador, a young Spaniard, and no longer yearned for her older lover. She became magnificently moody and duplicitous, which for Dostoevsky was all the justification needed for believing that love always involves pain. Falling on his knees and desperately clutching her legs, he acknowledged he had lost her, while she found she had been betrayed by Salvador, who had supposedly fallen ill with typhus and yet suddenly confronted her as large as life on the street. Furious at being rejected, she threatened to kill him. In this bitter mood she was ready to accept Dostoevsky's proposal that they treat each other as siblings rather than lovers on the next stage of their holiday, which involved a visit to Italy.

Arthur Schopenhauer

First of all he had to satisfy his gambling fever and hopefully boost his funds. Visiting Baden-Baden for the purpose, he called on Turgenev who had gone to live there after the hostile reception of *Father and Sons* and, more aptly, because he sought to be close to his beloved Pauline Viardot. They discussed Turgenev's prose poem *Phantoms* (*Prizraki*), which was promised to Dostoevsky's journal, and his recent interest in the pessimistic philosophy of Arthur Schopenhauer (1788–1860). The sombre tone of this visit was compounded by Dostoevsky's careful avoidance of any mention of his travelling companion, since he knew only too well that Turgenev would gossip. Money, meanwhile, was lost at roulette, watches and jewellery had to be pawned and the Italian visit became beset by worries over hotel bills. A brief encounter with Herzen and his family in Naples may have been intellectually stimulating, but emotionally and sexually the trip was proving a disaster. Polina still hankered after her young Spanish lover and was determined to return to Paris. Finally they parted in acknowledgement that there was no mutual passion left. Dostoevsky was not going to leave his wife, as Polina had hoped, and being his mistress had lost its appeal. Yet he would never forget Polina, the first real love of his life, and he would immortalize her in such portrayals of capricious *femmes fatales* as Nastasia Filippovna in *The Idiot* (1868–9) and Grushenka and Katerina Ivanovna in his last novel, *The Brothers Karamazov* (1879–80).

After two and a half months abroad, seriously in debt due to another gambling spree at Bad Homburg, Dostoevsky returned to St Petersburg and immediately left for provincial Vladimir, where his wife was in the final stages of tuberculosis. As for his literary future, official permission had been obtained to publish a new journal, *Epoch* (*Epokha*), but the hope that it would lead to a recovery of his fortunes soon proved unfounded. The new journal was never able to attract either a sufficient number of noteworthy contributors or enough subscribers and, hostile to some of the extreme views expressed in the more radical *The Russian Word* (*Russkoe slovo*), it undeservedly acquired an unduly conservative reputation. Since it depended largely on its literary appeal, *Epoch* could offer little of importance apart from Turgenev's *Phantoms* and Dostoevsky's own contributions, but he was more concerned with his wife's deteriorating health and moved to Moscow to be with her. In the course of his long vigil at her bedside he wrote *Notes from Underground* (*Zapiski iz podpol'ia*, 1864).[38] It is now recognized as the most seminal of his post-exile works and proved to be the only important thing *Epoch* ever published.

The significance of *Notes from Underground* relates as much to the past as to the future of Dostoevsky's evolution as a writer. The first part, the Underground Man's confession of the paradox of his existence, could be said to refer to his 40-year-old self, while the second part – a short story entitled 'Apropos of the wet snow' ('Po povodu mokrogo snega') – illustrates his confession by reviving memories of what happened when the narrator was 24. This 24-year-old *persona* of the Underground Man recalls the idealistic dreamers of Dostoevsky's work of the 1840s, but imperilled in his case by the way his ego is entangled in a paradox of assertiveness and humiliation, private megalomania and public self-abasement. He has a chip-on-the-shoulder persecution complex which makes him long to dominate others, but leads to farcical confrontations and only serves to emphasize the gap between his grandiose dreams and the squalor of his relationship with Liza, a young prostitute. In a brilliantly realized encounter between them, Liza is evoked very fully as a character despite being portrayed only from the Underground Man's point of view. She may once have been impressed by his bleeding-heart concern for her welfare, but she finally reaches the sensible conclusion that his feeling is really one of hatred. She forces him into an awareness of his own egoism and ultimate misanthropy. He never imagined, for example, that she would not take his money and dashes out into the snow after her only to reach his own cynical conclusion about her egoism of suffering. 'Which in the end is better,' is the question he poses as the moral of his experience, 'a shoddy happiness or an exalted suffering?'

The Russian Word was notorious for publishing the iconoclastic work of Dmitri Pisarev (1840–68) who praised the character of Bazarov in *Fathers and Sons* very highly and also, as a spokesman for his own kind of nihilism, advocated the abolition of aesthetics and all institutions that supposedly stood in the way of progress. He was an amusing and elegant polemicist.

The deeper meaning of this sad little story can only be understood in the light of the Underground Man's confession in the first part. Afflicted with toothache, malevolent, resentful, isolated in his urban bolthole, this 40-year-old 'superfluous man' was intended to be representative of *a still living generation*,[39] so Dostoevsky claims in a footnote. More than this, he achieves a universal human relevance from the way that Dostoevsky's ironic diagnosis of his condition (a semi-satirical attack on Chernyshevsky's 'rational egoism') became the template for so many of his future novelistic heroes.[40] Essentially he is a man consumed by the paradoxes of the egoism of suffering in the context of the new ideas of the 1860s. For the Underground Man humanity is divided very roughly into those who aim bull-like straight at their target in life and those who are mice. He aspires to be a bull, but being hypersensitive, he is really no better than a mouse, so that when he is faced with the stone wall of science – meaning the laws of the natural sciences expressed most eloquently in the rigid formula $2 + 2 = 4$ – he seeks to avenge himself upon such deadly rigidity by asserting that humanity is not rationally inclined to act in its own best interests, as Chernyshevsky had assumed. No, protests the Underground Man, the more supposedly rational and civilized humanity pretends to be, the more bloodthirsty it has become. Human beings seek to demonstrate their individuality, their egoism, by the exercise of caprice, by free will, by wanting (*khotenie*), by striving towards an absolute individual freedom, for it is only through the assertion of free will that individuality can be guaranteed.

The type of the 'superfluous man' (*lishnii chelovek*) was first fully delineated by Turgenev in *The Diary of a Superfluous Man* (*Dnevnik lishnego cheloveka*, 1850) and this type has long been regarded as the literary ancestor of Dostoevsky's Underground Man.

For this reason humanity will never become a plaything of the laws of the natural sciences. When the Crystal Palace of the mathematically perfect society has been created along utopian, socialist lines and humanity has become as regulated as ants, human caprice will dissent. For, according to the Underground Man's wickedly cynical, yet irreproachably fair assessment: *In a word, man is comic; the whole thing's a bloody joke. Yet twice two is four is still absolutely bloody awful. Twice two is four is, in my view, merely sheer bloody effrontery. Twice two is four looks like some bastard who stands in your way with his hands on his hips and spits. I agree that twice two is four is an excellent thing, but if we've got to praise every bloody thing, then twice two is five is also sometimes a nice little item.*[41]

This uncompromisingly honest view of human contrariness must mean that humanity will inevitably reject the shoddy happiness promised by social utopians and will never turn away from real suffering, from destruction and chaos, because suffering is doubt and negation, something that a rationally ordered society must necessarily banish from life. In the light of a century and a half's experience since Dostoevsky wrote these lines in the name of his Underground Man, humanity has learned to experience more wars and bloodshed than at any other period in its history. But this was not intended to be Dostoevsky's final message. It may well be that he was prevented by the censors from including a section about the need for faith which reflected some of his profound notebook musings written beside Marsha's corpse a day after her death in mid-April 1864.

Dostoevsky would always be, as he put it in his famous letter to Fonvizina, *a child of the age, a child of disbelief and doubt*,[42] but what he most feared was the possibility that human life on earth would turn out to be senseless and the universe without meaning. He looked then to Christ as a permanent ideal, a Christ, that is to say, who entered fully into humanity, for humanity was always striving to be transformed into the *ego* of Christ as its ideal. Here, however, there is a tragic paradox: *Humanity strives on earth towards an ideal* opposed *to its nature. When humanity has not fulfilled the law of striving towards an ideal, that is to say has not* through love *sacrificed the* ego *to others or another being (I and Marsha), it feels suffering and has called that sin. Consequently, humanity must ceaselessly experience a suffering which compensates for the heavenly joy of having fulfilled the law by sacrifice. That is earthly equilibrium. Otherwise the earth would be senseless.*[43]

To embody this paradox of a humanity striving to achieve an ideal opposed to its nature – not merely in terms of the dialectic employed by the Underground Man, but in terms of a fully delineated characterization, in terms of a hero – now became Dostoevsky's principal endeavour. It was adumbrated in the Underground Man's final exhortation to his readers not to be frightened of becoming human with their own *personal* body and blood rather than aspiring to be some model of universality. *We are still-born*, he wrote, *and for quite a while now we've not been born of living fathers, and we're finding this more and more to our liking. We're getting a taste for it. Soon we'll think of a way of being born of an idea. But enough of this; I don't want to write any more 'from the Underground' . . .*[44]

The pretentiousness of liberalism as exemplified by the idiotic General Pralinsky in 'A Nasty Story' ('Skvernii anekdot', 1862) or the radicalism lampooned in 'The Crocodile' ('Krokodil', 1865) are instances of Dostoevsky's readiness to caricature such still-born ideas. Amusing though they are, the laughter comes through tears. He did not want to write more anecdotal work of this kind. There were tears of overwhelming grief to be faced. They sprang from his immediate future and darkened his prospects for a decade.

Crime and Punishment

Within three months of his wife's death in April 1864, Dostoevsky's brother Mikhail died, exhausted by the effort of keeping *Epoch* afloat. The shock of the deaths of the two people closest to him left Dostoevsky in utter despair, as he explained to his friend Baron Wrangel:

And there I was suddenly all alone, and it was simply awful. My whole life had been split in two. In the one half that I had already passed through was everything I had lived for, and in the other half, the unknown half, everything was strange and new and there wasn't a single living soul that could take the place of the two of them. Literally – I had nothing left for which to live.[45]

To abate the sense of desolation he threw himself into his work. Unwisely, but courageously, he took on all of his brother's debts as well as others, used money from his mother's family to help his brother's family and devoted himself night and day to keeping the journal alive for as long as possible. It soon became obvious that all his efforts could do no more than postpone the inevitable and the last issue of *Epoch* came out in March 1865. The debts piled up, for which Dostoevsky assumed full responsibility, and until the 1870s he lived under a cloud of financial worries. He was forced to beg for funds from all manner of sources, always to his shame, and, more shamefully still, became

Epoch left its mark in a limited sense on Russian literature, since it not only published Dostoevsky and Turgenev, but also *Lady Macbeth of Mtsensk* (*Ledi Makbet Mtsenskogo uyezda*, 1865), a remarkable story by Nikolai Leskov (1831–95), plus the work of the poet and critic Apollon Grigoriev (1822–64), whose untimely death contributed further to Dostoevsky's distress.

closely acquainted with the grubby world of St Petersburg moneylenders.

Understandably, widower that he was (though not exactly fancy-free), he indulged himself with some smart new clothes and engaged in flirtatious, possibly sexual relationships with several much younger women. One was Martha Brown who had joined the staff of *Epoch* on a temporary basis. Married to a sailor from Baltimore, she had lived in England for a while, but had returned to her native Russia when the marriage ended. She and Dostoevsky worked together and were apparently on close terms, but the relationship seems to have petered out by 1865 when he became interested in a young girl, Anna Korvin-Krukovskaia, who had contributed short stories to the journal. Dostoevsky's relations with her stuffy, half-German family proved difficult. His courtship of Anna and the accompanying ambience may be reflected in Myshkin's wooing of Aglaia in *The Idiot*. Anna had no intention of marrying him and he tended to distance himself somewhat by seeking to be treated as a celebrity in his own right.

Editorship of *Epoch*, if not in his name, had at least given him a modest circle of acquaintances as well as a great deal of work. Desperate for funds after its closure, he offered a plan for a novel called *Drunkards* (*Pianitsy*) to Kraevsky. When refused, he reluctantly accepted a draconian agreement with the unscrupulous publisher Stellovsky. Against an advance of 3,000 roubles Dostoevsky agreed to complete a new novel by the end of November 1866, otherwise he would forfeit all right to payment for everything he might write over the following nine years! With this additional threat hanging over him and such funds as he had raised already distributed among creditors, he went abroad in late July 1865 with fewer than 200 roubles in his pocket. It was his earnest hope to improve his health and have time to write, but most of all he planned to cover his debts by winning at the gaming tables of Wiesbaden. Five days later he had lost everything.

He had to swallow his pride and seek a loan from Turgenev on the promise of repayment within a month. Turgenev could afford only 50 thalers against the 100 Dostoevsky had asked for and the promised month for repayment ran into years, inevitably blighting their friendship. Dostoevsky was meanwhile reduced to penury. Polina Suslova visited him briefly and then, in her flighty way, left him alone to face the indignity of a deeply disapproving German hotel management. Refused food, confined to his room and with only poor quality tea to sustain him, he had reached rock bottom. By some miracle far more munificent than any roulette wheel he conjured into being a plan for a masterpiece. Equally miraculously, the plan has been preserved for posterity in a draft letter to Katkov, editor of *The Russian Messenger* (*Russkii vestnik*) proposing what he called a short novel (*povest'*) about *the psychological account of a crime*:

The action is contemporary, in the present year, he wrote. *A young man excluded from university, petit-bourgeois by origin and living in extreme poverty, frivolously, shaky in his grasp of things and submitting to certain strange 'unfinished' ideas that are floating around in the air, has decided to get out of his miserable situation at one fell swoop. He has decided to kill an old woman, a civil servant widow who lends money. The old woman is stupid, deaf, sick and greedy, charges Jewish rates, is evil and ruins other people's lives, turning her younger sister into a skivvy. 'She's no good.' 'Why should she live?' 'Is she of any use to anyone?' These questions drive the young man out of his mind. He decides to kill her and rob her in order to make his mother, living in the provinces, happy and to save his sister, who is a companion in a noble family, from the lustful attentions of the head of the family, attentions which threaten her life . . .*

He spends almost a month after the crime before the final catastrophe. He is not suspected and cannot be. It is here that the whole psychological process of the crime unfolds. Unresolved questions arise before the murderer, unsuspected and unexpected feelings torment his heart. The truth of God and the law of nature come into their own, and he is finally forced *to give himself up . . .*

Apart from that, my short novel hints at the idea that the judicial punishment imposed for such a crime frightens a criminal a lot less than lawgivers think because he himself morally demands it.

I have seen this even in the most immature people, in the crudest instance. I have wanted to express this idea in the case of an educated man, a man of the new generation, so that the idea can stand out more clearly and conspicuously.[46]

These are the beginnings of *Crime and Punishment*. It seems likely he may have conceived the idea for it in Siberia and had most certainly been pondering the psychological process and the 'unfinished' ideas throughout the 1860s. It is equally certain that he did not conceive the work initially as a long novel. It grew over the months of composition into the extended six-part work, replete with epilogue and a large cast of characters, that we know today through the addition of material intended for *Drunkards* and the development of subplots. But he offered enough in his letter to Katkov for the latter to agree to an advance.

In fact, though this money helped, what enabled Dostoevsky to escape from the straitened circumstances of the Wiesbaden hotel and the threat of a debtors' jail was money from Baron Wrangel and some help from Father Yanishev, a priest at the local Orthodox church. On the return journey to St Petersburg Dostoevsky stopped off for ten days in Copenhagen to see Wrangel, who had proved a true friend, and they reminisced about their time in Semipalatinsk. Back in St Petersburg Dostoevsky spent the final months of 1865 in relative seclusion, busy drafting his novel, though it was not until November, it seems, that what had originally been conceived as a first-person narrative became a third-person one.[47]

Still short of money and forced to beg for more loans from

Katkov, Dostoevsky took heart from the response to Parts I and II of *Crime and Punishment* (*Prestuplenie i nakazanie*) when the serialization began in *The Russian Messenger* in January 1866. Enormous interest was aroused by his portrayal of a young university drop-out who displayed so many characteristically nihilist features. Dostoevsky's reputation as a leading writer was immediately enhanced – and his appeal to the younger generation endorsed – by the attention he received that summer when he spent some time in the company of young students and their friends on a relative's estate near Moscow. He found himself both a centre of attention and a lively, much appreciated participant in their games and discussions. In tones of serious banter, as if echoing Pisarev's iconoclasm, the issue of whether boots were more important than the works of Pushkin was vigorously debated. Dostoevsky was intrigued by the younger generation's obsession with nihilist ideas, but he could also make fun of them in ribald doggerel. What he could not make fun of was his epilepsy and his novel. The combination gave rise to the stationing of a servant by his bedroom in anticipation of a seizure and led to the servant's adamant refusal to continue his vigil because he was so alarmed by Dostoevsky's habit of pacing up and down at night muttering about murder.

Dostoevsky's gothic doodles in a draft of *Crime and Punishment*

Crime and Punishment, a novel about murder, has the distinction of differing significantly from most other examples of crime fiction by concentrating on the murderer's motives rather than his identity. The opening paragraph establishes the tone. An anonymous young man leaves his tiny rented room in a five-storey tenement and walks the hot St Petersburg streets at the beginning of July. We do not know why he counts the 730 steps to his destination, why he is so unused to human company, why his slightly incoherent short passages of interior monologue sound like private mutterings, a dialectic conducted with the self. He can be seen as experiencing inner tensions externalized in a dramatically tense account of his actions and state of mind akin to hypochondria: his fear of meeting his landlady, his hunger, his impoverishment, his ragged clothes, his battered hat.

The references in his thoughts to *it*, a *test* (*proba*), to something involving courage and disgust, the deliberate concealment, in short, helps to heighten the tension much as his outward poverty is sharply at odds with his remarkable good looks. Above all a sense of peril in urban St Petersburg is enhanced by his own solitariness in the midst of the dust, the building work, the heat, the special smell of the city in summer, the busy street noise. Such tensions between his solitude and the self-compromising participation that human contact demands of him are reflected not only in his name, Raskolnikov (or 'one who is split in two'), first revealed to the moneylender, but also in the duality of his motives as exposed stage by stage throughout the ensuing narrative. For *Crime and Punishment* can be regarded as brilliantly constructed on the tension between *pro* and *contra* in determining whether Raskolnikov is a criminal or not.

By so centring the novel upon the experience of Raskolnikov it has been claimed that Dostoevsky achieved a remarkable unity of time, place and action.[48] The unity of time – never to be precisely gauged owing to Raskolnikov's periods of unconsciousness – probably amounts to little more than two weeks. The dramatized chronology tends to enlarge a minute into an hour and turn a day into an important item in a lifetime. Time, as a stasis, has little role to play in carrying the fiction forward; while the place is manifestly St Petersburg and the particular area around the Haymarket (*Sennaia ploshchad'*) where Raskolnikov lives. There can be no doubt that by amalgamating the plot of his proposed short novel *Drunkards* into Raskolnikov's story and blending it with the issue of his own family and the plight of his sister Dunia (as anticipated in the original letter to Katkov) Dostoevsky created two subplots that, in part, accompany and help to illuminate the hero's dilemma. As a study of the 'psychological process' of Raskolnikov's crime the novel naturally involves motive; and this in turn requires a dramatic postponement of the likely cause of the hero's psychological state. But the true greatness of *Crime and Punishment* lies in its credibility as an anatomy of murder in which the reader is left to guess not who committed the murder but why.

At the conclusion of Raskolnikov's 'experimental' visit to the moneylender, Alena (pronounced 'Al*yo*na') Ivanovna, the sun shines with menacing brightness into her little room (so immaculately kept by her wretchedly overworked half-sister), as if exposing the bloody crime that Raskolnikov's dialectics will oblige him to commit there. Immediately afterwards he visits the basement tavern, the haunt of solitaries like Marmeladov who seek to purge their egoism of suffering in confessions similar to that made by the Underground Man. Marmeladov's confession makes reference to his daughter, Sonia, who has taken the yellow ticket of prostitution, and the conviction that an all-merciful God could provide universal forgiveness for the sins of humanity – and for a Raskolnikov as well, we may assume, whose last day in the novel, in Sonia's company, is dominated by the conviction that *in place of dialectics life had emerged, and something completely different had to be worked out in his mind.*[49]

In other words, the ending of the novel, in terms of its moral, is anticipated on the very first day, but the action of the novel is concerned with the struggle between dialectics and life as played out

The scene of the crime. Nikolay Karasin's illustration for *Crime and Punishment*

in Raskolnikov's consciousness. By the time he has set out to complete his 'experiment' much has been revealed about his past, be it through his mother's lengthy letter and its references to various people or through a student's remark overheard while passing through the Haymarket. The latter instance sheds a simplistic light on Raskolnikov's motives. In reference to Alena Ivanovna, the student says: *'Kill her and take her money* [. . .] *For one life thousands of lives saved from decay and degeneration. One death and a hundred lives – that's simple arithmetic! And what, when weighed on the scales of all things, does the life of this consumptive, stupid and evil old woman mean? No more than the life of a louse or a beetle . . .*[50]

Such ideas are similar to Raskolnikov's and are sufficiently shocking to revive his fever and force him into a prolonged sleep. Murder as the equivalent of insecticide could be said to trivialize the idealism of his dialectics and to emphasize both his immaturity and the clear association between sickness and crime. Other incongruities similarly emerge in his decision to use an axe rather than a knife, to use the butt rather than the blade to kill the old woman, to kill her half-sister as well and to escape detection by a favourable convergence of coincidences so grippingly described by Dostoevsky.[51] On the face of it Raskolnikov had committed the perfect murder.

What appals us about the murder and the preceding events is the powerful evocation of detail in an almost cinematic sense; for instance, the excited, exclamatory manner of the dialogue, the 'suddenness' of actions, the exploration of Raskolnikov's state of mind through nightmares and the awful documentary banality of killing the old woman: *Her bright, thinnish hair streaked with grey, as usual thickly plastered with grease, was plaited into a rat's tail and fastened by a bit of horn comb that stuck up on the nape of her neck. The blow struck the very top of her skull, helped by her short stature. She cried out but very weakly and suddenly slid to the floor, though she managed to raise both hands to her head. She still kept hold of 'the pledge' in one hand. Then he struck again and again with all his force, again using the butt, again hitting the top of the head. Blood poured out as if from an overturned glass and the body collapsed backwards.*[52]

As a murderer, Raskolnikov can hardly be described as evil. Enough is known about his background and character for others to be drawn to him, much as one might expect provincials on arrival in the capital to be drawn to one of their own, but he is in any case an attractive personality. Razumikhin is his only real friend, though they have not seen each other for four months. He sees in Raskolnikov what his name implies: a man alternating between two opposed characters. Others are intrigued by him, even at the police station to which he is summoned immediately after the murder – not as a suspect, but for unpaid debts, a clever means of increasing the tension. He at once sets about hiding the goods he has stolen. The original object of using them for his family has become redundant.

Part of the novel's dramatic power resides in the fact that those closest to Raskolnikov can hardly be aware of his real, private darkness. By dismissing Luzhin, one of his sister's suitors, Raskolnikov quickly disposes of a simplified sort of 'rational egoism', but a kind of demoniacal pride makes him confess his crime in mocking terms and revisit the murder scene. Marmeladov's involvement in a street accident and subsequent death brings into play the relationship with Sonia and the possibility that, through her influence, Raskolnikov might renew his life; just as, returning to his room and being confronted by his mother and sister who have recently arrived in St Petersburg, he can only acknowledge that his plans for their welfare have come to nothing. Within a short while, he has persuaded himself – and been persuaded by Razumikhin – to walk of his own volition into the camp of his enemy, Porfiry Petrovich, the investigator of the murder.

At this point (Part III, Chapter 5) the first true revelation of motive occurs. It hinges upon an aspect of Raskolnikov's past that has hitherto been concealed, even in part from himself: the publication two months previously in a periodical of a short review article entitled *On Crime* that he had written six months before when he left the university. His synopsis of it, and Porfiry's comments, cover such matters as the psychological state of the criminal during the criminal act, the accompanying sickness and the division of humanity into two general categories of 'ordinary' and 'extraordinary'.[53] Of the two, the 'extraordinary' was the Napoleonic model, for, as Raskolnikov goes on to explain: '*I hinted quite simply that the "extraordinary" man has the right . . . that is, not an official right, but he himself has the right to permit his conscience to overstep . . . some barriers, and solely if the enactment of his idea (sometimes perhaps capable of saving the whole of humanity) should demand it.*'[54]

The central notion is that ideas have a right to be acted on. The ideas of Kepler and Newton demanded to be known to all humanity and Newton would have had a right to exterminate whoever opposed their dissemination, since, by the same token, certain benefactors and leaders of humanity (Lycurgus, Solon, Mahomet, Napoleon) had created new laws by transgressing the ancient ones, of ancestral origin, held sacred by society. In so doing they became criminals, usually by the bloodiest of means. There is nothing new in this, reasons Raskolnikov. The mass of people are 'ordinary', material to be manipulated by the few 'extraordinary' people, since the latter have the gift and the talent to utter a new word and drive the world forward towards a New Jerusalem – in which, incidentally, Raskolnikov confesses he believes under Porfiry's questioning, just as he confesses to believing in God and the raising of Lazarus. Raskolnikov insists, in other words, that ideas must be enacted, that the Word should become flesh, not necessarily as a protest against the abnormality of the social order or for any supposedly altruistic purpose, but, as Razumikhin sees it, as a justification of bloodshed *in the name of conscience*.[55] Yet, in Raskolnikov's view, conscience can only admit to pain as a condition of existence when experienced by the truly great or the erstwhile Napoleonic men of free will.

The exact opposite is immediately demonstrated to him when, after being accused of murder by a stranger in the street, he rehearses to himself the genesis and justification of his former thoughts. The ensuing nightmarish reconstruction of his crime and his frenziedly laughing victim reveal the sickness of his conscience. Out of it, in an awful coalescing of the subconscious and the real, emerges the menacing progenitor of his illness in the form of his sister's stalker and predator, Svidrigailov.

As a latter-day demon. Svidrigailov exerts a malign fascination. Inscrutably sensual, young-looking, with a handsome, mask-like face and sky-blue eyes, the very embodiment of shabby grandeur, Svidrigailov exudes seediness. His artificial grandiloquence has a parodic subtext. He is attractive to Raskolnikov both as his sister's suitor and stalker and, more sinisterly, as a demonic parody of the Napoleonic motive through his nihilistic denial of everything save sensual gratification. Possibly a wife-murderer, menaced by hauntings, Svidrigailov seems to guess instinctively, as an emanation of the nightmare his life has become, that Raskolnikov is guilty and can be suborned by this knowledge into sacrificing his sister.

What follows is magnificently frenzied. In going to Sonia's misshapen room (adjacent, somewhat remarkably, to Svidrigailov's), Raskolnikov has to make a choice between acceptance of guilt and possible resurrection on the pattern of Lazarus or cynical defiance of such humility in the name of achieving power over all trembling creation; between, that is to say, Sonia's belief and Svidrigailov's arrogance. An air of tragic farce now pervades the novel and culminates in Marmeladov's funeral feast, the only extended *skandal* scene and a *tour de force* of comic bravura. Afterwards, feverishly, as if purging himself of his dialectics and vomiting out his guilt like a poison, Raskolnikov returns to Sonia's room and forces himself to admit that he is neither a Napoleon nor a benefactor of humanity and that something else made him commit the two murders: '*I had to know something else, something else nudged me to do it: I had to know, know right away, was I a louse like everyone else or was I a man? Could I overstep the law or couldn't I? Did I dare stoop down and pick it up or not? Was I a trembling creature or did I have the* right . . .'[56]

His intellectual arrogance, based on his dialectics, makes him refuse Sonia's plea to confess in public and yet has its counterpart in the last frenzy of Marmeladov's widow, Katerina Ivanovna, who similarly refuses to humble herself at the end. The resolution of Raskolnikov's dilemma comes as a consequence of encounters with the figures now most nearly concerned with his guilt – Razumikhin, Porfiry, Svidrigailov and Sonia. Razumikhin (the name, based on *razum*: 'intellect') sees in Raskolnikov either madness or political conspiracy. Porfiry, the urbanely insinuating investigator, has guessed his guilt, commending his article for its boldness and suggesting in so many words that his choice lies between accepting life and divine forgiveness on the one hand, or, on the other, taking his own life. It is at this stage that Svidrigailov's role assumes a crucial importance. In passages of surreal and nightmarish horror, after confronting Dunia and melodramatically escaping her intended bullet, Svidrigailov spends a final night afflicted by hellish visions before ending up on the banks of the Neva. Asked by a grotesquely helmeted figure what he is doing, he answers that he is going to foreign parts, to America. Then he shoots himself.

Only one choice now remains for Raskolnikov if he wishes to live and so he makes public obeisance, on Sonia's insistence, and confesses. Sentenced to seven years in Siberia, where Sonia joins him, he can hardly be regarded as a totally reformed criminal. His motives for the murder prove false or inadequate at each point of revelation and his guilt is in no sense properly mitigated even by confession. He remains arrogant. For Dostoevsky, the 'psychological process' of Raskolnikov's crime is symptomatic of a sickness of apocalyptic dimensions. Raskolnikov has become infected, it would seem – or so his final delirious dream suggests in mockery of his dialectics – by a plague from the East that drives people mad: *But never, never before had people considered themselves so intelligent and unshakable in the knowledge of truth as these infected people considered themselves. Never had they considered more unshakable their right to pass judgement, their scientific conclusions, their moral convictions and beliefs.*[57]

The promise of regeneration is given at the novel's conclusion in fairy-tale hope, but the world of *Crime and Punishment* and of the St Petersburg depicted by Dostoevsky is in so many senses unregenerate; and Raskolnikov himself is profoundly symptomatic of the choices nineteenth-century humanity had to make in order to achieve moral regeneration. Dostoevsky created an urban world of such vivid reality in his St Petersburg, so redolent of the squalor associated with incipient capitalism and its distorting effects on human expectations and happiness, that no image of city life in nineteenth-century literature can rival it. Raskolnikov's characterization may represent an initial stage in Dostoevsky's examination of the very particular Russian phenomenon of nihilism, but in creating this multifaceted portrait he plumbs aspects of human pathology unknown, on the whole, to Victorian sensibilities and produces a remarkably modern, remarkably universal type. At the heart of the first of Dostoevsky's great novels, the portrait of Raskolnikov leaves in its wake taxing and largely unresolved questions, while the novel itself has shown an unparalleled power to infect and excite its readership over generations. *Crime and Punishment* can be regarded as the most carefully constructed, the least like a 'fluid pudding', as Henry James described the Russian novel, of any of Dostoevsky's great works.[58]

Like his hero, Dostoevsky was also in need of regeneration, if not morally, then in terms of a change of personal fortune. It was literally out of *Crime and Punishment*, or between the commission of the crime and the administering of the punishment, that this change occurred. The novel proved popular from the moment of first publication and each new part of the serialization was awaited eagerly throughout 1866, earning Katkov's *The Russian Messenger* several hundred new subscribers in the process. The novel's topicality was immediately recognized. Not only were there newspaper reports of murders matching Raskolnikov's, but in April of that year the issue of murder became of national importance when a young ex-student, Karakozov, attempted to assassinate the Tsar while he was returning from his customary stroll in the Summer Gardens. Immediate governmental repression led to the final closure of *The Contemporary*, since Karakozov was supposed to have been influenced by the journal's radicalism. In Dostoevsky's case, a temporary hiatus in the publication of his own work became necessary for another reason. He had to meet Stellovsky's draconian deadline for the completion of a new novel before 1 November.

Dostoevsky 1860 portrait

He gave himself barely a month in which to complete the task. At first it seemed impossible. He declined offers of collaboration, feeling it should be his own work, and finally decided on employing a stenographer. Dictation was a risky and untried method for him. When the 20-year-old Anna Grigorievna Snitkina, star pupil of a stenography course, arrived at Dostoevsky's apartment on 4 October, she was as much in awe of the well-known writer as he was apprehensive about this kind of gamble: he immediately began dictating much too fast. The novel was, in any case, to be entitled *The Gambler* (*Igrok*) and Dostoevsky was as uncertain about the way it should evolve as he was unused to this way of working.

By planning at night (it had become his habit to write largely at night) he was soon able to achieve regular daytime dictations, which Anna took home with her and copied out in final form for the next day. The novel progressed quickly in scarcely more than three weeks. Probably improved by the rapidity of its composition, as a study in the addictive power of gambling *The Gambler* spins out its tale with the ease of a roulette wheel. A first-person narrative subtitled *From the Notes of a Young Man*, it recounts the experiences of a certain Aleksey Ivanovich in a fictional Roulettenburg and particularly his relations with a capricious but attractive woman, Polina Aleksandrovna. The relationship is evidently autobiographical and tinged with sadness in its exploration of mutual misunderstandings, but well sustained passages of dialogue and lively characterization help to make the novel light but agreeable reading and doubtless offered its author a welcome change of mood from the psychological anguish of Raskolnikov. Equally, there can be no doubt that the young narrator's flawed character may well have revealed more about its author to the impressionable stenographer than Dostoevsky supposed. As a novel with a non-Russian setting and several non-Russian characters – notably a well-drawn and relatively sympathetic portrayal of an Englishman, Mr Astley[59] – *The Gambler* offers a foretaste of Dostoevsky's preoccupation with Western influences; limited, in this case, to generalizations about national characteristics and a sprinkling of easily understandable French phrases.

By dint of dictation and Anna's assiduous copying *The Gambler* was finished before the November deadline. Dostoevsky was able to obtain proof of the novel's submission well within the time limit despite the wily Stellovsky's attempt to enforce a breach of contract by deliberately absenting himself from St Petersburg. More importantly, the wheel of fortune had swung decisively in Dostoevsky's favour. In the course of dictating *The Gambler* he fell in love with his young stenographer, a feeling which was reciprocated, to his great joy, despite the quarter of a century difference

St Nicholas Cathedral in St Petersburg

in age; and it was to Anna that he dictated the closing pages of his first true masterpiece, *Crime and Punishment*.

Second Exile. *The Idiot*

In Anna Snitkina, Dostoevsky found a girl 25 years his junior who had remarkable common sense and practical ability, though she may never have understood the true extent of his genius. He knew that in her he had found his little diamond, as one of his dreams foretold. She laughed off this extravagant idea by comparing herself to an ordinary stone. Ordinary, perhaps, in that her Swedish inheritance on her mother's side and the Ukrainian on her father's endowed her with pleasantly strong features, fair hair and attractive grey eyes, but not ordinary at all in her possession of a life-saving devotion that could turn her love for a man more than twice her age into a pearl beyond price.

Anna Dostoevsky in 1868

Dostoevsky's proposal of marriage came in the form of a story he wrote for her entertainment. She was so impressed she accepted and the couple were married in a lavish ceremony in the Izmailovsky Cathedral in February 1867. Earnings received from the publication of *Crime and Punishment* in a separate edition and an advance against a future novel meant he could afford to be generous, but his young bride was horrified to find him so affected by the excitement and the champagne that he had two epileptic fits in quick succession. Her new husband writhing and howling in pain was shock enough, but, more worryingly, the importunate demands of his widowed sister-in-law and family, as well as his sponging step-son Pasha, emphasized the extent to which they had battened on him for support and resented her as an interloper. Other creditors, hitherto content to receive interest, now demanded full or partial repayment. Appalled by the threat of imprisonment for debt and the way Dostoevsky's earnings had been so eroded, Anna sold part of her dowry to pay for a trip abroad as the only means of escape. It would be a kind of delayed honeymoon lasting three months. In fact, when they took the train from St Petersburg on 12 April 1867, *en route* to Berlin, they never imagined they would be leaving for more than four years of exile.

Dostoevsky took strong exception to Berlin on arrival and the couple quickly moved to Dresden where they rented a small apartment. Soon the gambling mania returned. He felt certain he could improve their finances by winning at roulette and, in May, went to Bad Homburg to try his luck. The result, as one might have expected, was a succession of ruinous losses resulting in desperate letters full of recriminations and pleas for money to Anna in Dresden. She tolerated her husband's weakness of will, provided it did not also extend to renewal of his relationship with Polina Suslova. Dostoevsky had received letters from her, which left Anna feeling desperately jealous and insecure. She need not have worried. By July, having moved to Baden-Baden, he was able to claim in writing to his mother-in-law that he had never been happier in his life than he was with her daughter.

The visit to Baden-Baden was less happy in other respects. Information about this period of his life can be gleaned mostly from his correspondence with Apollon Maikov and, naturally enough, a principal topic was xenophobia, especially directed at the Germans and Swiss. Dostoevsky was particularly appalled by

Russian expatriates who denigrated their own country. Of these the most celebrated was Ivan Turgenev, already a long-term resident of Baden-Baden, who had compared Russia culturally to no more than smoke, as his latest novel was entitled (*Dym*, 1867). Dostoevsky had not wanted to meet him – 50 thalers was, after all, still owing – but when he did finally pluck up the courage to receive what he called Turgenev's *farcically aristocratic embrace with which he pretends to kiss you but offers you his cheek instead* the account he gave of the meeting was admirably acid.[60]

Turgenev deeply resented the hostile reception his novel had received and apparently claimed that if Russia disappeared from the earth there would be no sense of loss, not so much as a ripple across the face of humanity. Russians, he claimed, should seek to emulate the Germans and Europe; he was planning, he said, a long article attacking Russophilia. Incensed, Dostoevsky retorted that he should order a telescope from Paris. Why? *'It's a long way off,' I answered. 'You should point your telescope at Russia and study us carefully, otherwise it'd be hard to make us out.'*[61]

However annoying this sally was, Turgenev grew even angrier when his guest wondered aloud what civilization had done for ordinary people in Europe and why they had the right to boast about it. At this his host went white, according to Dostoevsky, expostulated that he felt personally insulted by the remark, was now a resident in the West and was proud to be considered German rather than Russian. So staggering was this statement that Dostoevsky apologized for any insult and left Turgenev's house vowing never to set foot in it again.

The quarrel became famous not only because it ended all personal contact between two of Russia's greatest writers, but also because it can be taken as marking an obvious line in the sand between the idea that Russia should learn politically and culturally from the West and a more potent, if romantic, notion that Russia was spiritually Europe's superior and, possibly, its saviour.

At the heart of this divide, in Dostoevsky's view, was Turgenev's avowed atheism and the atheism of so many so-called Westernist liberals of his generation, chief among them Belinsky. Dostoevsky had been commissioned to write an article entitled 'My Acquaintance with Belinsky' at this time, and it may well be that in thinking about this influential critic, as Joseph Frank has suggested, he came face to face with the issue of a Russian Christ and the image of his new hero, Prince Myshkin; for it was Belinsky's mockery of Dostoevsky's attachment to Christ that probably caused the rift between them in the 1840s.[62] Most certainly, on moving to Geneva and encountering both Herzen and Ogarev,[63] Dostoevsky made no bones about his hostility towards liberals and atheists and caricatured the activities of the left-wing Congress of Peace and Freedom that was being held in Geneva at the time. Indeed, it seems more than likely that in planning his new novel he was aiming to attack more firmly than ever the demonic arrogance, as he saw it, of such types of nihilism as he had already portrayed in Raskolnikov.

One event concentrated his ideas wonderfully. On their way to Geneva he and Anna had stopped off in Basel and paid a visit to the local gallery. A painting by Holbein the Younger depicting the dead Christ as a corpse so shocked him that he believed such an image could undermine the faith of the most devout believer. To one who relished the tension between opposites, this seemingly atheist or humanist image of the Son of God as irrevocably dead both appealed to his mystical need for a renewed and risen Christ and heightened his sense of the depth of evil that the world faced without such a redemptive faith. The search, however, for a means of encompassing this in fiction was by no means easy, as his notebooks for the last few months of 1867 demonstrate by their extraordinarily complex jottings.

Dostoevsky began one version of his projected novel and promised Katkov to have it ready for *The Russian Messenger* by January of the following year, only to abandon it completely and start on a new novel on 18 December. Having almost gone mad, as he confessed to Maikov, he finished the first five chapters by 5 January and sent them off, but remained unsure what exactly he was writing. He had begun, as he said, to grapple with a new type of hero: *For a long time I have been tormented by an idea, but I had been afraid of turning it into a novel because the idea was too difficult and I wasn't ready for it, although the idea was completely seductive and I was in love with it. The idea was* – to depict a completely beautiful man. *Nothing could be more difficult than this, in my opinion, particularly in our time.*[64]

Almost simultaneously, at the beginning of 1868, he was able to be a little more explicit about his intentions. Writing to his relative Sonia Ivanova, he stated that *the novel's main idea is to depict a positively beautiful man*,[65] a task made doubly difficult by the fact that only the Christ of St John's gospel had truly embodied beauty and European attempts to depict an equivalent ideal in such figures as Don Quixote and Mr Pickwick had been beautiful because they were comic, since the arousal of compassion in the reader is the secret of humour. Naturally, in view of Dostoevsky's repeated assertion of Russia's spiritual superiority to Europe, the ideal he had in mind would be Russian, yet flawed and, after a fashion, idiotic.[66]

It would reflect, with tragic irony, the single most significant event that occurred during the writing. In March 1868 Anna gave birth to their first child, Sonia, and it was, in Dostoevsky's words, as if *the soul of an angel had flown down to us*.[67] The devoted parents loved their baby to distraction and planned to leave Geneva to go to Vevey on the other side of the lake in the belief that it would be healthier there, but before the move could be made baby Sonia contracted an inflammation of the lungs, was ill for a week, seemed to improve and then suddenly died. Dostoevsky was heartbroken.

Oh, Apollon Nikolaevich, he wrote to Maikov, *suppose my love for my first child was silly, suppose I was silly in expressing myself about her in so many letters to those who sent their congratulations. For them I was the silly one, but to you, to you I'm not frightened of writing. This little three-month-old being, so poor, so tiny, was already for me a person and a character. She was beginning to know and love me and smiled whenever I approached. Whenever I sang songs to her in my silly voice, she loved hearing them. She did not cry or frown when I kissed her and she would stop crying when I came close. Now they comfort me by saying I can have more children. But where's Sonia? Where is this little person for whom I am bold enough to say I would suffer the agony of crucifixion if only she could be alive?*[68]

His angel had died and the tragedy of it darkened the message of his novel. The bereaved parents were inconsolable. They moved to Vevey shortly after the baby's death in May, but Dostoevsky felt more cut off than ever from current Russian affairs through lack of access to newspapers and journals. Moreover, he began to suspect that the St Petersburg police were opening his correspondence. Vevey itself was dull despite the scenery and he and Anna fell ill. They decided to move to a warmer climate. Shortage of funds, a constant refrain in his letters, meant that all moves would have to be conducted as cheaply as possible, so the journey across the Alps to Italy was made largely on foot, though in good weather. Milan, their initial destination, proved rainy, their circumstances monastically austere, and by the end of 1868 a further move had been made to Florence. Meanwhile, by slow stages, Dostoevsky's second great novel was emerging.

The Idiot (*Idiot*, 1868–9) can be regarded as the boldest in conception of all Dostoevsky's great novels and the most like a 'fluid pudding'. Bold in the sense that it aimed to depict a latter-day Christ in the figure of the 'idiot' hero, the epileptic Prince Myshkin (*mysh* suggests 'mouse'); its resemblance to Henry

James's uncomplimentary 'pudding' came about through its pamphlet-like preoccupation with nihilism, liberalism and a range of different issues. The magnificent opening scenes of Part I and the climax of Part IV do not wholly compensate for poorly achieved and often somewhat ludicrous moments in the novel's central narrative. All is redeemed, however, by the sustained fluency of the writing and the aura of genius surrounding the characterization of the prince himself. Carried through tidal waves of loquacity and improbability to the ultimate murder and madness of the ending, the reader has to accept, as Dostoevsky insisted, that the novel's real meaning resides precisely in its climax.

It is by this token a disaster novel, meaning that its promise of regeneration in the aim of portraying 'a positively beautiful man' could never rise above the apocalyptic vision of a world consumed by money and greed. Light and dark pervade relationships in a kind of dialectic, paradoxically informing portraiture as much as ideas and producing a dramatic tension of opposed impulses in all the principal characters. Most obviously this can be seen at the opening of the novel when Myshkin and Rogozhin encounter each other in the Warsaw–St Petersburg express and at the end when they appear to become twin but opposed aspects of the same passion in their final vigil beside the murdered body of Nastasia Filippovna. This tragic and powerful ending reveals the real meaning of *The Idiot*. In Rogozhin's case as murderer, his whole portrayal is cloaked in darkness like his house, like his reproduction of the Holbein picture, like his assumption that money can buy love. Myshkin, on the other hand, can only regress into the idiocy of his past sojourn in Switzerland from which he had sought, in his regenerated state, to bring to a corrupt St Petersburg a luminous gospel of beauty as the world's salvation. Few ideas in literature have the majesty, however flawed, of Myshkin's message and none shine with such simple and childish innocence; yet, for him as for Dostoevsky, there is an inescapable awareness that he is alien to the world's beauty, to the luminosity of spirit that he seeks to impart. It is expressed in a moment of recollection during the first year of his treatment:

He was then still an idiot, did not even know how to speak properly, sometimes could not understand what was being asked of him. One time he went up into the mountains on a clear sunny day and walked a long way thinking out some tormenting and ever elusive idea. In front of him was the gleaming sky, below him the lake, all around him the bright and unending horizon without limit. He gazed at it and suffered agonies. He now recalled how he stretched out his arms into this bright, endless blue and wept. It tortured him to think he was a complete stranger to it all. What was this feast, what was this great everlasting festival that had no end and had always drawn him to it, from his very childhood, and of which he could never be a part?[69]

It is, in one sense, the image of the 'poor knight' from Pushkin's poem[70] that Aglaia reads out at the Epanchins (Part I, Chapter 7). His cry is *Lumen coeli* ('Light of heaven'), the messianic cry proclaiming defeat to the Mussulmans, though his crusade ends with the poem's laconic admission in the last line that he died insane. In another sense, Myshkin's love of the light is inseparable from love of the European feast of which he can never be a part, perhaps also as Dostoevsky had loved the same 'great everlasting festival' since childhood, but could never join it, strictly speaking, and therefore grew hostile to it. Or in the sense that Myshkin's love is essentially twofold, projected in the ideals of Aglaia, the charming but capricious girl who seeks love and marriage, and Nastasia Filippovna, who seeks forgiveness for her 'egoism of suffering' as a fallen woman and recognizes the prince's compassion, but knows it is not enough.

Her portrait is one of the most memorable that Dostoevsky ever drew. Mistress to the wealthy Totsky, Nastasia repudiates all attempts to buy her love and, in the dramatic *coup de théâtre* of a climax to Part I, challenges her intended, Gania Ivolgin, to plunge his hands into the flames to seize the money from Rogozhin that she has thrown there. No matter how melodramatic such a gesture is, it sets in relief all the venality and corruption of the St Petersburg world to which her life has been sacrificed. Nastasia's wounded pride has at its core a craving for the vision of moral renewal she finds in the childlike prince and what illuminates her inner being is her own image of a Christ isolated from disciples in a world of fading daylight:

A child would be playing beside him, perhaps telling him something in its child's language and Christ would have listened, but now became thoughtful; his hand would be resting idly, forgetfully, on the child's bright head. He would be gazing into the distance, at the horizon; a thought as great as the whole world would fill his eyes; his expression would be sad. The child would fall silent at that instant, lean on his knees and, supporting a cheek with one hand, raise his head and pensively, as children sometimes do, look fixedly at him. The sun would be setting . . . That's my picture![71]

The picture is sentimental, no doubt, and suitably Victorian, but it represents a diamond in the urban darkness of shuttered rooms, such as Rogozhin's, where Nastasia dies. Myshkin's own message is just as concerned with death. In his initial speeches he confesses to an empathy for those facing the guillotine as well as the firing squad, as Dostoevsky had done, not to mention his defence of the child Mary during his Swiss exile. What he has to say is always confessional, but so uttered that it evokes the kind of sympathy reserved for an intelligent and sensitive child. Nowhere in Dostoevsky's work is the onset of an epileptic seizure described so fully as in Part II, when the prince, after an absence of some months, wanders in the environs of St Petersburg in early summer and experiences what Dostoevsky himself had been experiencing with increasing frequency whilst writing his novel – an *inner* light that lit up his soul: *The moment lasted perhaps no more than half a second, but he nevertheless recalled clearly and consciously the start, the very first sound of the terrible howling that was torn from his breast of its own accord and he had no power to stop. Then his consciousness was instantly extinguished and complete darkness descended.*[72]

This description of an epileptic attack is a metaphor for the prince's destiny. He has an inner light – Dostoevsky's genius achieved this much insight into his hero's being – and does indeed howl out his final message, but the end is the darkness of his returning idiocy. The opposition he faces is projected most clearly not in the venality of the surrounding world, nor in the somewhat simplistic political ideas offered by various subsidiary characters, but in the consumptive student Ippolit Terentiev's long peroration about death, *My Necessary Explanation (Après moi le déluge)*.

Symbolic of evil for him is the nightmarish creature he imagines in his room, the poisonous scorpion-like reptile of which even the dog Norma is apprehensive. This 'mystery' he cannot explain. In all essentials, though, his explanation amounts to an indictment and a challenge. As an indictment, it anticipates the devastating critique of God's world made by Ivan Karamazov in Dostoevsky's last novel and his reasons for returning his entrance ticket. As a challenge, it poses a question about the meaning of Holbein's portrayal of the dead Christ. If, in short, *death is so awful and the laws of nature are so strong, how can one overcome them? How can one overcome them when they are not overcome now by him who overcame even nature when he was alive, which submitted to him, who cried out 'Talitha cumi!' and a girl arose from the dead and 'Lazarus, come forth!' and he who was dead came out.*[73]

Ippolit's explanation is, in the end, an *apologia* for his intended suicide, since in the face of such apparently incontrovertible forces as Darwinism all hope for change is rendered pointless and suicide becomes *the only thing that I could still succeed in starting and finishing of my own will.*[74]

It is suitably ironic that he fails to end his life as he had promised, at the approaching dawn, but his deeply pessimistic analysis of the human condition has about it the same powerful charge as the Underground Man's confession of self. The prince's role similarly acquires a different emphasis in the novel's final part, when his childlike insouciance becomes submerged beneath a sermonizing tendentiousness. The shock of the news that his benefactor has become a Roman Catholic provokes a howl of derision against Roman Catholicism as an un-Christian religion and the source of atheistic socialism. He opposes it with his call for the emergence of a Russian Christ and his assertion that he has returned to Russia to meet his own class, the true princes of Russia. He will sit among his peers and they, the princes, will become the true leaders of a morally rejuvenated nation. As a sermon containing some of Dostoevsky's most cherished views, it is ironically accompanied, first, by the breaking of a precious Chinese vase, then, after the prince has proclaimed his joy in living, by his collapse in an epileptic fit to the alarm and bewilderment of his concerned listeners. The idiocy is incipient, in other words, even at this most crucial moment in his destiny; and if his message is little appreciated, so is his readiness to marry Nastasia Filippovna.

But the last word is not with the prince, it is with Madame Epanchin. On visiting the prince in Switzerland when he has already regressed into complete idiocy, she pronounces her eminently sensible, if domestic, verdict on a Europe that does not know how to bake bread properly and where everyone freezes in winter like mice in a cellar: '*We've had enough fun for now, it's time to be sensible. All this, all this place abroad, all this Europe of yours, it's all a fantasy, and all of us who are abroad are living out a fantasy. Mark my words, you'll see I'm right!*'[75]

Madame Epanchin doubtless speaks with Dostoevsky's voice when she offers her xenophobic verdict, and yet the voice is not, strictly speaking, hate-filled so much as mocking. A novel full of an extraordinary poetry, even in the rhythms of the often protracted speeches, with characters of interest despite their eccentric and sometimes improbable behaviour, *The Idiot* has throughout a vein of attractive whimsy that appeals to the reader. The childlike central portrait might all too easily have become sentimental and shallow, but encased as it is in a sensitively written novel graced with remarkable maturity of understanding and love, it acquires a stature morally superior to everything Dostoevsky had achieved thus far.

The Devils

However unintended, Prince Myshkin's initials, L N (Lev Nikolaevich), were the same as Count Tolstoy's and intimated a rivalry between the two leading Russian writers that Dostoevsky consciously nurtured at this point in his career. Aware that Tolstoy's epic novel *War and Peace* (*Voyna i mir*, 1869) had earned a popular success surpassing his own with *The Idiot* and dealt, even if it were principally a fiction, with the first major confrontation between Russia and Europe in the nineteenth century, Dostoevsky laid plans to match its importance with a rival work about Russia's spiritual relationship to Europe. Although initially entitled *Atheism*, it gradually evolved into notes labelled *The Life of a Great Sinner* (*Zhitie velikogo greshnika*),[76] in the sense of a saint's life or a hagiography, designed to explore the spiritual dilemma of the contemporary Russian intelligentsia when confronted by European ideas and the atheism at the heart of nihilism.

By the spring of 1869 Dostoevsky was becoming heartily sick of his enforced exile in the West and sick of Florence, even though he had enjoyed the Uffizi, the Boboli Gardens and other features of that famous city. To fulfil his ambition for an epic novel he dearly needed to return to Russia. He kept apart from his compatriots in Florence, because the single most significant object of his enmity was the type of wealthy Russian that lived abroad. They were, in essence, more devilish and treacherous at heart, in his eyes, than the native Russian nihilists he had depicted in his two previous novels. But lack of money – especially the failure of a new magazine called *Dawn* to pay him in advance for a promised contribution – meant that Dostoevsky and Anna (now in the later stages of a second pregnancy) were obliged to remain in Florence during the torrid heat of the summer. Only in July did sufficient funds become available to allow them to start once more on their travels.

Their aim was to move to Prague where it seemed likely there would be better access to Russian newspapers and journals. In any event, Dostoevsky was very anxious for Anna's health in her pregnancy and sought a healthier climate. They moved first to Bologna, then to Venice. St Mark's was greatly admired among other aesthetic delights. Finally they travelled via Trieste to Prague. Three days of searching persuaded them that there were no suitable apartments for rent and so, rather than try expensive France, they returned to Dresden. They stayed for 20 months from mid-August 1869. Here, Dostoevsky was to write *An Eternal Husband* (*Vechniy muzh*) and begin his novel *The Devils* (*Besy*). Here also Anna gave birth in September to a daughter, Liubov or Liuba and Lalia for short (1869–1926), their first child to survive into adulthood.

Fedya and Liuba

By the end of 1869, with the baby healthy and family contentment more certain, Dostoevsky's life in Dresden acquired a strict routine. He worked at night, which had always been a habit of his but now both guaranteed him peace and apparently helped to stave off epileptic attacks. Rising at about midday, he would work again for a couple of hours between 3 and 5 p.m., then take a half-hour walk to the post office, always returning by the same route. The family would then have dinner. At seven o'clock he would again go out for a stroll, then return and, after the Russian ritual of tea-drinking, he would set to work about half past ten and work through until 5 a.m.

The twofold making of plans for a further novel and the actual writing of his novella *An Eternal Husband* kept him fully occupied at this time, not to mention the regular correspondence conducted with his niece, Sonia, and his friends Maikov and Strakhov. From these sources we have glimpses of Dostoevsky's plans and constant reminders that his principal concern was lack of money. Help in a practical sense came with the arrival of his mother-in-law to look after the baby. More significant was the visit in October 1869 of his young brother-in-law, Ivan Snitkin, a student at the Petrovsky Agricultural Academy in Moscow. Through him Dostoevsky was very likely given an insight into events at the Academy that were to have tragic results and were to inspire him to write his most controversial novel, *The Devils*.

Meanwhile, in *An Eternal Husband* he created the most sophisticated, sardonic, well-constructed and, in the Dostoevskian canon, least likely work to be expected of him at such a time. As a study of a relationship between two men supposedly opposed to each other as superior and inferior, it obviously has a typically Dostoevskian theme, but of a complexity in non-ideological terms and a stylistic maturity that matches and outshines even the work of such masters of the genre as Turgenev or Henry James. Velchaninov, a self-possessed philanderer, gifted in the ways of seduction, though introspective by nature and consumed by doubts, finds himself stalked by a certain Trusotsky, an 'eternal husband' whose hurt at having been cuckolded by the other man is ironically embodied in his daughter, Liza. The father's love-hate for her might be assumed to show his odious character, although the complex triangular relationship between father and supposed daughter and Velchaninov (in the absence of DNA the actual paternity has remained uncertain) causes richly emotional scenes of conflict, misunderstanding and tragedy, especially when Liza dies. The climax comes when Trusotsky attacks Velchaninov with a razor and cuts his hand. The latter fights off his assailant and ties him up, but eventually releases him, only to become captive to his own bad conscience when he reads a letter from Trusotsky's dead wife revealing the truth about his affair with her and confirming Liza's true parentage. In a delightfully ironic epilogue the 'eternal husband' and the 'eternal lover' have a brief encounter at a railway station two years later when it becomes obvious that the recently remarried Trusotsky is about to be cuckolded again and Velchaninov recognizes, perhaps to his own chagrin, that his sole role in life is to be a seducer, despite all of his elaborately neurotic self-analysis.[77]

If a single meaning can be adduced from such an ironic treatment of the age-old theme of the cuckolded husband, it may well be that it highlights Dostoevsky's ongoing concern with the Great Sinner as a type epitomizing the ideal of self-conquest and therefore the exact opposite of the protagonists in his story. For although *An Eternal Husband* was the story promised to *Dawn*, he was also frantically engaged in planning what he described as a five-volume work to rival Tolstoy's which needed a particular type of hero. Meanwhile, his financial state reminded him of Dickens's Mr Micawber, faced as he was with the likelihood that Stellovsky was republishing *Crime and Punishment* apparently for nothing. The yearning for Russia, a recurrence of epileptic fits and increased anxiety over the state of Europe with the outbreak of the Franco–Prussian War led to ever greater aversion towards the Eurocentric or Westernist attitudes of his own generation of the Russian intelligentsia, meaning in particular such figures as Belinsky, Turgenev and their immediate predecessor, Chaadaev.

P Ia Chaadaev (1794–1856) was the first Russian to offer a reasoned critique of Russian cultural backwardness in his famous *Philosophical Letter* (1836), originally written in French and first published in a journal temporarily under Belinsky's control. Probably the most contentious of his criticisms was that Russia had received Christianity from the 'corrupt' source of Byzantium, whereas Western Europe had evolved culturally under Roman Catholicism and to this extent was superior. Declared mad by the authorities, he published his *Apology of a Madman* (*Ispoved' sumasshedshego*, 1837) in which he modified some of his criticisms, but insisted that he would never love his country blindly, only as Peter the Great had taught him to love it. In other words, he wished by and large to see Russia more amenable to Western influences. Although officially silenced, he remained a 'living reproach' to the autocracy for the last 20 years of his life.

Dostoevsky's search for a new theme and type of hero for his projected novel received added impetus from what has come to be known as the 'Nechaev affair'. His brother-in-law may have mentioned a certain Ivanov during discussions about political unrest among fellow students at the Petrovsky Agricultural Academy in Moscow. Initially attracted by revolutionary ideas, Ivanov was said to have changed his mind in protest at the control exercised over the small revolutionary cell to which he belonged. It therefore came as a shock to Dostoevsky to learn from newspaper reports in late 1869 that Ivanov had been murdered and his body thrown into a pond. The alleged instigator of this murder was a certain Sergei Nechaev who had escaped abroad, leaving in his wake a smokescreen of rumours about his activities as a revolutionary organizer that provided ample material for reports and articles in the Press. Nechaev had ordered the murder of Ivanov, it was said, to ensure the loyalty of other members of the revolutionary cell. Such facts, often elaborately embroidered and inevitably unreliable, preoccupied Dostoevsky to the extent of lending his intended fiction a basis in fact of the kind familiar to us from Tolstoy's masterpiece *War and Peace*. Dostoevsky's concern with fact was essentially topical rather than historical, but none of his novels relies more obviously on fact than *The Devils*.

The extent to which the young Ivan Snitkin provided inside information about Nechaev's activities and therefore helped to colour Dostoevsky's subsequent portrayal of the revolutionary activists in his novel – particularly of Petr (pronounced P*yo*tr) Verkhovensky – is the subject of some dispute. In a letter to Katkov of October 1870, accompanying the dispatch of the first half of the Part One of his novel, Dostoevsky hastened to make clear that *neither Nechaev, nor Ivanov, nor the circumstances of the*

Nechaev (1847–82), born in the textile town of Ivanovo, educated himself sufficiently to study in Moscow and St Petersburg and eventually became a teacher. Towards the close of the 1860s, in the wake of Karakozov's attempt to assassinate the tsar in 1866, Nechaev created a reputation for himself as a revolutionary activist responsible for organizing revolutionary cells throughout Russia and, in 1869, he collaborated with Bakunin in Geneva to produce the extremist revolutionary document *The Catechism of a Revolutionary*. Shortly afterwards he returned to Russia and became involved in agitation and organization at the Petrovsky Agricultural Academy. He then returned to Geneva, but he was thought to have fraudulently appropriated revolutionary funds. Denounced to the authorities in 1872, he was incarcerated in the Peter and Paul fortress in St Petersburg, where he succeeded in converting his guards to socialism. A regime of greater severity imposed after the assassination of Alexander II in 1881 led to his death from scurvy a year later.

murder are known to me and I know nothing about them apart from newspaper reports.[78] This may not mean, of course, that he knew nothing about these matters from his young brother-in-law; it may simply mean that, sensitive as he was about his convict record, he naturally sought to counter any possible objections or suspicions about the likelihood of his access to inside knowledge, especially on so politically sensitive a topic.[79] In any case, the direction Dostoevsky's new novel assumed in the wake of what became known as the 'Nechaev affair' was essentially political and it concentrated on the politics of the Russian intelligentsia as they had evolved since his own involvement in revolutionary politics in the 1840s.

Added to the political impulse for the novel was an apocalyptic sense that European influences had begun to have a demonizing effect. In an interesting letter to Maikov written a day after the letter to Katkov he set out to explain the meaning of his projected work as explicitly as possible. A recent article in the Russian press had shocked him by asserting that certain sections of the liberal intelligentsia probably welcomed the successes of the allies in the Crimean War.

No, he wrote, *my liberalism never went that far; I was then in penal servitude and did* not *rejoice at the success of the allies, but along with other comrades of mine, 'unfortunates' and soldiers, I felt myself a Russian and wanted success for Russian arms but – though I still had even then a strong taste for mangy Russian liberalism of the sort propounded by f***ers like the dung beetle Belinsky and others – I did not consider myself illogical in feeling Russian. True, facts have also shown us that the epidemic affecting civilized Russians was a great deal worse than we imagined and the matter didn't end with the Belinskies, Kraevskies and others.*[80] *But at this point something happened to which Luke the evangelist has borne witness: There was a man possessed of devils and his name was Legion and they begged Him to let them into a herd of swine and He suffered them. Then went the devils out of the man, and entered into the*

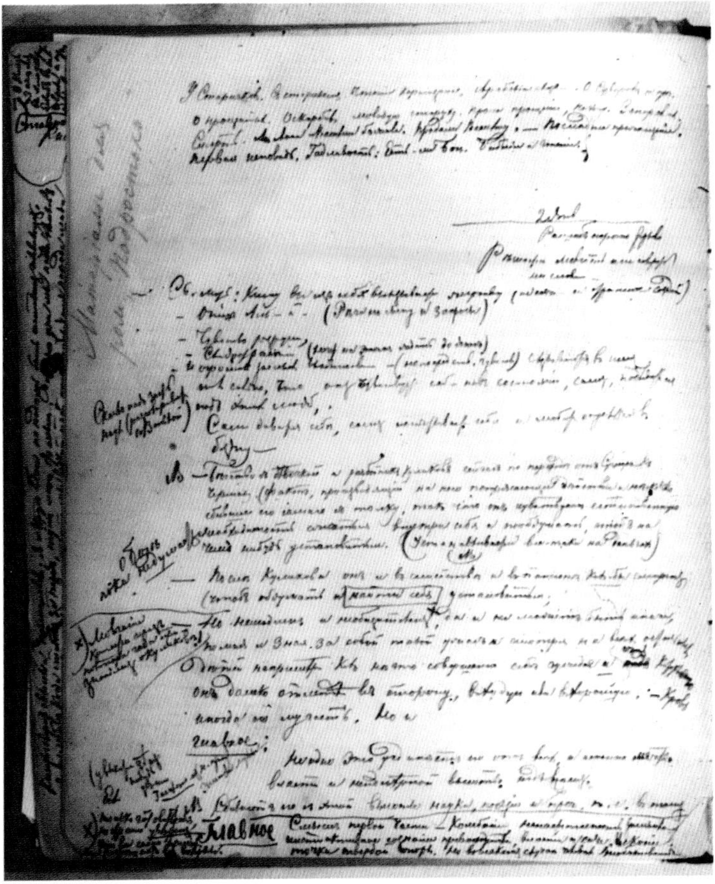

Dostoevsky's additions on a draft page from *The Devils*

swine; and the herd ran violently down a steep place into the sea and were drowned. When the people from the surrounding area ran to see what had happened, they saw the man formerly possessed of devils sitting at the feet of Jesus, clothed, and in his right mind, and those who had seen it all told them how the man possessed of devils had been healed. That is exactly what has happened with us. The devils have gone out of Russian man and entered into a herd of swine, that is to say into the Nechaevs and the Serno-Soloveviches and others.[81] *They have drowned, or will certainly drown, and the man made whole, from whom the devils have gone out, is sitting at the feet of Jesus. And that is how it should be. Russia has been spitting out the filth it has been fed and of course there is nothing Russian left in the scoundrels that have been spat out. And take note, dear friend: whoever loses his people and his nationality also loses his faith in his country and his God. Well, if you want to know, this is the theme of my new novel. It is called* The Devils *and it describes how these devils entered into a herd of swine. Without doubt I'll make a mess of it because, being more of a poet than an artist, I always choose themes beyond my powers.*[82]

This letter embraced by and large the gamut of meaning and emotional commitment that Dostoevsky brought to his new novel. If it was to be about the way in which new ideas relating to socialism and the notion of universal human contentment were able to take possession of human beings and challenge the idea of God, then the search for God and the purpose of life were as much part of its hidden agenda as they were an acknowledged aim for Tolstoy's heroes Andrei Bolkonsky and Pierre Bezukhov in *War and Peace*. Had Dostoevsky been permitted to publish the chapter 'At Tikhon's' as he had intended, the novel's meaning in this respect would doubtless have been clearer. Although the impulse for *The Devils* was obviously patriotic, the apocalyptic and biblical lesson to be learned from it soon enough acquired a prophetic meaning. No work of nineteenth-century literature issued a more cogent warning to the twentieth century about the corruption and manipulation of social ideals in the name of political power than *The Devils*.

It was the first of Dostoevsky's major novels to have a provincial setting (thought to be Tver, where he was initially permitted to reside after returning from Siberia) and a narrator. As a means of distancing himself from his subject matter Dostoevsky used a *faux-naïf* narrator, a local chronicler who tends to keep a straight face even when purveying the most outrageous tit-bits of gossip. In passages of dialogue Dostoevsky often dispenses with this artifice or the narrator's presence is simply hard to explain, yet as friend and confidant of Stepan Trofimovich Verkhovensky the chatty narrator is party to much tittle-tattle in chronicling the activities and personalities of the eccentric little group surrounding this gentleman, as well as his relations with one of the richest local ladies, Mme Stavrogina, owner of the Stavrogin estate of Skvoreshniki.

Stepan Trofimovich becomes tutor to her son, Nikolay Stavrogin. What he teaches is not specified in detail. His excitable, delightfully bombastic manner, leavened with French phrases, ridicules the Western-oriented pretensions of the first generation of the Russian intelligentsia. At heart he preserves what he refers to as 'a great idea' that has become *'a plaything of stupid boys'*,[83] meaning that the principles of freedom and justice espoused by his generation have been distorted and debased by the 'Sons'. In this case the son means Nikolay Stavrogin.

The adult Stavrogin becomes the central figure of *The Devils*. His precise nature, if he has one, remains unclear to the bitter end. Previously known in the district three years earlier (so the narrator claims), he had become notorious for a number of pranks. Pronounced mad, he had gone abroad. Upon returning to the present time of the fiction, he is in his late twenties, handsome, charismatic and in all essentials an enigma. His mask of a face exemplifies the nihilistic idolatry so necessary as a focus for all revolutionary fanaticism and yet he is a false God, a 'pretender' (*samozvanets*), one emptied of any princely heritage, a man called Legion dispossessed of his devils.[84]

It has to be assumed that ideologically his devils have gone out of him and found a lodging in two of his supposed 'disciples',

Shatov and Kirillov. Among his first acts upon returning to his native town is to pay night-time visits to his 'disciples' (Part II, Chapter 1) as if he is somehow reliving the darkness of his past. Kirillov is a visitor like himself, an engineer trained in the building of bridges, but infected by the notion that he can overcome humanity's need for a bridge to God by committing suicide in order to demonstrate, as the narrator has learned from him, that *'God is the pain of the fear of death. Whoever will conquer pain and fear will himself become God.'*[85] Somewhat mockingly, Stavrogin asks him at their meeting:

'You love children?'

'I do,' Kirillov responded, though rather indifferently.

'So that means you love life too?'

'Yes, I love life too, so what?'

'If you've decided to shoot yourself?'

'What of it? Why put them together? There's life – it's separate, so is the other. Life is, but death isn't.'

'Have you begun to believe in a future eternal life?'

'No, not in a future eternal life, but in an eternal life here and now. There are moments, you reach certain moments and time suddenly stops and will stay stopped forever.'[86]

Yes, Kirillov, is to say a little later – and *The Devils* can be said to contain some of the most brilliant scenes of quasi-philosophical dialogue Dostoevsky ever wrote – he *did* stop time the previous week on Wednesday at 2.37 a.m., if only emblematically, in order to assert that whoever preaches such happiness on earth will be a Man-god, not a God-man. Stavrogin points out that the God-man sent as saviour to the human race was crucified. What he cannot acknowledge, it seems, is that Kirillov's scenario of humanity's recognition of its true virtue will brand him as someone who has raped a little girl and invoke his real guilt as a Great Sinner. He might well mock Kirillov as his disciple by claiming, in conclusion, that if he knew he would believe in God he would believe, but he didn't so he didn't; to which at the end of the novel Kirillov, on the eve of his suicide, replies that '*Stavrogin, if he believes does not believe he believes. If he doesn't believe, he doesn't believe he doesn't believe.*'[87]

Was Kirillov's idea merely one of Stavrogin's mad pranks? The question remains unanswered because, paradoxically, it seems he had simultaneously implanted in Shatov, his other disciple, an almost exactly contrary idea. It has been alleged that Shatov belonged to the 'secret society' formed in the town, but he denied the association. However, he knows Stavrogin's 'secret' – his marriage to the crippled Maria Lebiadkin – and he ostensibly slapped his face in public for this reason, although it is equally possible that his own wife's pregnancy is also at issue. Shatov's beliefs – derived, it seems, from Stavrogin – can be summarized as a search for God in the sense that '*The aim of every national movement, in every nation and at every period, is simply a seeking after God, its own God, expressly its very own, and belief in it as the one true God. A God is the synthesized personality of an entire nation from its beginning to its end.*'[88] Shatov therefore advocates the notion of Russia as a 'God-bearing nation' (*narod-bogonosets*), although when Stavrogin, again mockingly, asks him if he believes in God, Shatov can only answer 'I will believe', acknowledging hysterically that he is a man without talent, whereas Stavrogin is the one who should raise the banner.

This brief remark is the crux of the novel. It is from this point forward that Stefan Trofimovich's true son, Petr Stepanovich, newly returned from abroad, begins to assume a prominent place in the fiction. A supreme manipulator, not so much of ideas as of people, he represents the Dostoevskian version of Nechaev who is essentially concerned with power for his own ends and seeks to turn Stavrogin into someone who will raise the banner of Revolution.

The diabolism inherent in revolutionary politics receives its most cynical embodiment in Petr Stepanovich Verkhovensky. He argues, albeit jokingly, that to organize revolution one needs (1) uniforms, (2) sentimentalism (in order to believe in socialism) and (3) as a guarantee of cementing loyalty, '*the shame of having an opinion of one's own*.'[89] Opposed in his own 'revolutionary cell' by one Shigalev (pronounced Shigal*yo*v), who is adamant in declaring that, in studying the question of the structure of a future society, limitless freedom will end up as limitless despotism, Petr Stepanovich is ready to acknowledge this while cynically mocking it. For him, the realization of a completely equal society is to be achieved by abolishing all desire, whether for education or property; drunkenness, gossip and denunciation will be encouraged; for one or two generations depravity will be the order of the day and human beings will be transformed into foul, cowardly, cruel, selfish scum. Carrying the banner for this revolution will be Stavrogin as its figurehead.

Horribly prophetic though this may be of Stalinism, the cult of personality and the worst excesses of the Soviet period, within the novel such ravings might have seemed scarcely plausible had they not been driven by such implacable fanaticism. Petr Stepanovich began by ingratiating himself into the household of the newly appointed local governor, von Lembke, and his wife Julia, flattering them for their quirky little hobbies – in von Lembke's case, the writing of a novel and the making of a paper theatre and railway station – and, in Julia's, the organizing of a fête for poor governesses. He also befriends the famous writer Karmazinov, a bitingly unfair caricature of Turgenev, who is scheduled to read his latest work *Merci* (based on Turgenev's *Enough*) at the fête.

The Devils proceeds by stages from one *skandal*, one grandly operatic scene, to another. Of these probably the most hilarious is the speechmaking at the fête (Part III, Chapters 2–4) in which the demagogy of the most absurdly radical speaker vies with Stepan Trofimovich's attempt to argue a case for the priority of aesthetic standards.

The end of the party. Karasin's impression of the Ball scene in *The Devils*

'But I declare,' screeched Stepan Trofimovich in the ultimate degree of excitement, 'but I declare that Shakespeare and Raphael are above the emancipation of the serfs, above nationality, above socialism, above the younger generation, above chemistry, above almost all humanity because they are the fruit, the real fruit of humanity as a whole, the highest fruit there can ever be!'[90]

This leads to fiasco and culminates in pandemonium, accompanied by a riot among local workers, arson and murder. By the close of the novel all the principal characters save one are dead. Shatov becomes the Ivanov-like victim of Petr Stepanovich's machinations shortly after his wife has given birth; Kirillov is subsequently persuaded to sign a statement confessing to Shatov's murder shortly before committing suicide; Stavrogin hangs himself; Stepan Trofimovich embarks on a pilrimage among the peasantry and dies. Only Petr Stepanovich departs unscathed.

The melodrama of it all may seem to over-egg the message. The darkest, most bizarrely humorous and violent of Dostoevsky's works, *The Devils* offers little comfort in a spiritual sense except for the deathbed message of Stepan Trofimovich. Having discovered a belief in God, he pronounces a new truth to the effect that humanity wishes principally not for personal happiness but for the certainty of knowing and believing that somewhere or other there is perfect happiness: '*The entire law of human existence is simply that a human being should always be able to bow down before what is limitlessly great. If human beings are deprived of the limitlessly great, they will cease to live and will die in despair. What is without limit and without end is just as necessary for human beings as the little planet on which they live ... My friends, all of you: Long Live the Great Idea! The Eternal, Limitless Idea! Every human being, no matter who, needs to bow down before what is A Great Idea!*' [91]

Stavrogin is not part of humanity in this sense. When *The Devils* was completed in 1872, it did not contain the chapter 'At Tikhon's' ('U Tikhona'), because Katkov refused to publish it and Dostoevsky did not reinstate it in later editions. Published 50 years afterwards, in 1922, the missing chapter contains Stavrogin's *Confession*.

A sordid document, it describes in detail how, while living in St Petersburg lodgings, he had raped his landlady's daughter, Matriosha, a girl of 10 or 11. She had then hanged herself out of shame. So vivid is the account that it has a ring of authenticity. Whether or not it derives from Dostoevsky's own experience has never been proved. In any case, in showing this document to the priest Tikhon, Stavrogin may have sought forgiveness, even sympathy, for his 'Great Sin', yet the fact that he has already had the account printed suggests he sought to salve his sick conscience by confessing all in public. An acknowledged paedophile, then, as Kirillov intimates, Stavrogin carries with him the cross of eternal haunting by the vision of the wretched Matriosha raising her little fist at him in reproach.

On the other hand, he has an even greater cross to bear. He is an outcast from humanity because he bears the burden of an illusory dream about the Golden Age at the beginning of European civilization.[92] This was the curse of all Westernized Russians, Dostoevsky appeared to suggest. Stavrogin had this marvellous dream of a once innocent and idyllic world, but he knew it was no more than a grandiose illusion:

'*A dream, the most improbable of all the dreams there have ever been, to which all of humanity has all its existence devoted its strength, for which it has sacrificed everything, for which men have been crucified and prophets put to death, without which nations do not want to exist and cannot even die. I experienced all of this in the dream; I do not know exactly what I dreamed, but the cliffs and the sea and the slanting rays of the setting sun – all this I saw when I awoke and opened my eyes, which for the first time in my life were literally wet with tears.*'[93]

He can weep over the vanished dream of humanity's Golden Age even if he cannot expiate his own sin. The sinfulness of humanity, *The Devils* suggests, is inevitably the sole impediment to human advancement, let alone the achievement of A Great Idea.

Return to Russia

The Devils had not been completed by the time Dostoevsky returned to Russia in July 1871, but in one other respect his life had changed for good. In April, shortly before his return, with Anna's consent and using her carefully hoarded money, he went on a final gambling spree in Wiesbaden. As ever he lost everything. Bitterly ashamed and in despair, he swore he would never gamble again. This time he kept his word. The years of marriage and exile had made him aware how much he owed to his young wife. There was just enough money available to pay for their return and on 16 July, once on Russian soil, she could offer him no greater gift than the birth of a strong, healthy baby boy, their son Fedor (1871–1921).

Although the event augured well for the family's future, the Russia of the 1870s to which Dostoevsky returned faced changes of far-reaching consequence. Populism (*narodnichestvo*) had become the new ideal of the young intelligentsia. It was based on an idealistic belief that the peasantry or 'the people' (i.e. the *narod*) was the only force capable of offering genuine opposition to the autocracy. In the summer of 1874 several thousand young people participated in a spontaneous 'going into the people' in an effort to persuade the peasantry to achieve greater freedom. Hundreds of young Populists (*narodniki*) were arrested, largely due to peasant conservatism, and an impatient intelligentsia turned to terrorism instead. The People's Will (*narodnaia volia*), as the terrorist organization was called, soon began to attack the government directly. In foreign relations, Panslavism – the ideal of liberating Slav Christendom from Turkish rule – excited many messianic hopes during the decade. It culminated in the bloodshed and relative failure of the Russo–Turkish War of 1877–8, the first so-called 'war of liberation', just as Populist terrorism eventually ended in the bloody pyrrhic victory of Alexander II's assassination. To this decade of the 1870s, known as 'the epoch of great endeavours' (*epokha velikikh del*), Dostoevsky was to bear witness as both observer and prophet.

Tsar Alexander II. The Liberator of the Serfs who did not escape the assassin's bomb

He returned to take up residence in a variety of St Petersburg apartments over the coming 10 years, but beset as he still was by creditors, whom Anna successfully warded off, and still treated as a state criminal by the authorities, he sought peace for himself and his growing family by renting a summer villa in the tranquil surroundings of Staraya Russa not far from Novgorod. Later a house was purchased there and it became the family's regular holiday home. St Petersburg, though, was the centre of Dostoevsky's life as it was the seat of government and, due to the clear conservative bias in his views demonstrated by *The Devils*, he soon found himself befriended by such leading establishment figures as Prince Meshchersky, proprietor of the right-wing weekly *The Citizen* (*Grazhdanin*), and Pobedonostsev, tutor to the future Tsar Alexander III and shortly to be head of the Russian Holy Synod. With Pobedonostsev's help Dostoevsky gained influence at court, though his literary freedom remained dear to him and became increasingly precious when he was appointed editor of *The Citizen* at the beginning of 1873. At the

Dostoevsky's working table at Staraya Russa 1881

same time he and his wife independently published a separate edition of *The Devils* when it was completed in 1872 and quickly sold 3,000 copies.

It soon transpired that editorship of the weekly *Citizen* had serious drawbacks, even if it provided a regular income. Prince Meshchersky frequently interfered and the censors were unduly zealous in monitoring its contents. Such constraints, however irksome, did not prevent Dostoevsky from introducing his own views in a section he called *The Diary of a Writer* (*Dnevnik pisatelia*). It was hardly a diary as such, more a series of articles, and in terms of letterpress the longest work he ever published. It gave him freedom to maintain close contact with his readers, respond to their concerns and influence their ideas.

Reminiscences (among the first were items concerning Belinsky and Herzen, increasingly presented in a favourable light), comment on topical matters (crime, suicide, personal morality, the maltreatment of children, new literary works, the Eastern Question, etc.), xenophobia, anti-Semitism, patriotism, abhorrence of the petty intelligentsia, admiration for 'the people', genial bloody-mindedness, above all Christian commitment contributed to the rich journalistic mosaic of the *Diary*. The fecundity and vigour of the published material as well as the notes were astonishing. Dostoevsky continued it long after he had left his editorial post and, when published independently with his wife's help, it became a staple feature of his literary work, especially in 1876–7 and virtually to the end of his life. Nowadays it can be said to enhance his literary reputation chiefly through three short works of original fiction.

Of these *Bobok* (1873) is the least but in some respects the most intriguing.[94] A black satirical comedy based on voice hallucination, it involves a polyphony of corpses in a graveyard bandying words, often crudely, but in manifest denial of any spiritual afterlife. Longer and more moving is *A Gentle Girl* (*Krotkaia,* 1876), a 'fantastic story' in the form of an extended monologue by a successor to the Underground Man, in this case a money-lender grieving over the death of his 'gentle' wife. He had sought to dominate her by destroying her natural affection to the point where she tried to kill him with a revolver. When he had an eventual change of heart, she could not respond other than by throwing herself out of a window clasping an icon to her breast. Pessimistic, if psychologically acute, it is a soliloquy that plumbs the flawed character of the narrator and in this respect bears a resemblance to *The Dream of a Foolish Young Man* (*Son smeshnogo cheloveka*, 1877), another 'fantastic story' about a young man deterred from committing suicide through a chance encounter with a girl. The superb and daring irony of the young man's subsequent dream is that it mocks the idea of a Golden Age. He can admire and seeks to share the purity of the earthly paradise in which he supposedly finds himself, but his very presence there is like a sickness infecting and eventually corrupting it.

Dostoevsky's interest in suicide could always be considered morbid, but during the 1870s it had a basis in fact amply documented by reports in the press, particularly *The Citizen*. Suicide was symptomatic, in his view, of the turbulence of Russian society and the breakdown of the family. It became an abiding theme of his major work in the last ten years of his life, just as his own family grew larger and he became more aware of his parental responsibilities.

Simultaneously Dostoevsky began to achieve celebrity. The famous artist Perov painted his portrait. Those who met Dostoevsky may have seen a man of small build, thin but broad-shouldered, looking younger than his years, with small bright, brown eyes and, at first glance, an unattractive and ordinary face. 'But,' added one witness, 'that was simply an initial and momentary impression – the face immediately and permanently impressed itself on your memory through the imprint it bore of an exclusively spiritual life.'[95] Such was the mixture of ordinariness and profound spirituality that Dostoevsky projected. When he spoke in public or gave readings from his works, as he did with increasing frequency, it never failed to produce a remarkably dramatic effect. Meanwhile, the continuous grind of editorial work took its toll. Excessive smoking produced a diagnosis of pleural emphysema that required treatment at the German spa town of Ems in 1873 and again the following year. By the spring of 1874 he gave up his editorship, having been penalized through Meshchersky's carelessness to suffer imprisonment for a couple of nights as a result of infringement of censorship regulations. Exhausted, in poor health and at the mercy of epileptic seizures, he proposed to return to his true métier as a novelist.

Vasili Perov's portrait of Dostoevsky 1877

For some time, as his notebooks reveal, Dostoevsky had been contemplating a novel on the theme of 'fathers' and 'sons'. The result was *An Accidental Family* (1875),[96] his last completed novel and generally regarded as the least successful of his major works. It was published not by Katkov (who had committed himself to publishing Tolstoy's *Anna Karenina* and could not afford to publish Dostoevsky's novel as well), but by Nekrasov, editor of the left-wing journal *Fatherland Notes*, who had first published Dostoevsky's work 30 years before.

An Accidental Family is an extended first-person narrative by a 20-year-old looking for his true family. Arkady Dolgoruky has been born illegitimately to a princely name, although his 'spiritual' and legal father, Makar Dolgoruky, is no more than an estate serf married to a young wife, Sonia, whom the estate-owner, Versilov, has seduced through the exercise of his droit de seigneur. Abandoned by his biological father and given a perfunctory education, Arkady conceives the idea of achieving status by becoming as rich as Rothschild. His narrative opens with his arrival in St Petersburg armed with this idea and a letter with which to blackmail his father. In fact, he discovers in his father, Versilov, a type of cultured, Westernized intellectual (based on such prototypes as Chaadaev and Herzen) who intrigues and exasperates him and becomes his rival in love for Katerina Nikolaevna, the beautiful daughter of the amiably dotty Prince Sokolsky.

The novel, as this summary of its opening might indicate, is over-plotted in the extreme and the narrator, for all his raciness and brio in the telling, tends often to be ignorant of motive, unclear about the sequence of events, even unsure of names[97] and forever fortuitously eavesdropping or exercising an often implausible total recall. Arkady's commitment to finding his family may ironically have acted as a counterweight to ideas of suicide, since the two suicides described in the novel – that of Kraft whose self-image is shattered by his pathological belief that the Russians are a second-rate people, and that of Olia who kills herself largely because her insecure self-esteem is destroyed by Versilov's inept benevolence – result from a failure of 'idea-emotion', the notion of an idea as 'felt' that so absorbs Arkady.

Dostoevsky appears to be saying that Russian society is split between two counterbalancing concepts, between *bezobrazie* (ugliness, spiritual malformation) and *blagoobrazie* (beauty, nobility of soul), represented to a great extent by Arkady's two fathers and their respective backgrounds. Thus, Versilov's heritage of serf-ownership is caricatured in the portraits of the old Prince Sokolsky and his corrupt son Seriozha, who virtually disabuses Arkady of his ambition to be a Rothschild; whereas Makar Dolgoruky is an 'ideal' portrayal of a holy peasant (obviously influenced by Tolstoy's Platon Karataev in *War and Peace*) who has achieved a degree of nobility of soul through his pilgrimages across Russia. He proclaims the disavowal of riches and envisions a time to come when *'the earth will shine brighter than the sun, and there will be neither sadness, nor lamentation, but only a paradise beyond price.'*[98]

This vision of a paradise on earth contrasts with Versilov's version of an impossible Golden Age and his prophecy of universal citizenship. Essentially he is split in two like the icon he breaks – he is a Russian more European than the Europeans, consumed by his own double, in love with two women, yet also, as Arkady discovers, for all his peccadilloes and apparent fecklessness he has devoted all of his life to an idea. It is exactly an idea or 'idea-emotion' that Arkady seeks as much as he seeks his true father. His association with socialist groups (like those Dostoevsky had known in the 1840s) and the sleazy world of blackmail and extortion (exemplified by his friend Lambert), not to mention forgery and other criminal activities – all, incidentally, based on court cases and press reports – leads Arkady to respect all the more the notion of living for an idea. The most praiseworthy idea is personified by his mother, Sonia, whom Versilov has seduced, but whom Arkady loves deeply. Indeed, one of the great merits of this otherwise indifferent novel is Dostoevsky's sensitive portrayal of his female characters.

An Accidental Family ends melodramatically in a helter-skelter fashion, but the final idea it evokes is the most important of all: the need for order in Russian society based on traditional family life and the reconciliation of generations. In this respect, the young narrator challenges the Tolstoyan ideal of family life by being the product of what, for Dostoevsky, is far more typical of contemporary Russian life – an 'accidental family'. Through this chatty, aggressive, disconcertingly honest, chip-on-shoulder illegitimate narrator Dostoevsky aimed in his novel, as its final words declare, *to guess at the innermost spiritual world of someone on the eve of manhood* [. . .] *since it is from those on the eve of manhood that the generations are made.*[99]

The Brothers Karamazov

How the generations were made became critical for Dostoevsky towards the end of his life and provided him with the subject of his last novel. It was also one of his major concerns in his *Diary* of 1876–7, prompted by a desire to sympathize with the aspirations of the younger generation. It was no doubt partly due to the birth in 1875 of a second son, Alesha (pronounced Al*yo*sha, from Aleksei: 'Man of God'), and, more generally, to well-publicized court cases involving the gross mistreatment of children. Dostoevsky gathered information about the lives of children by visiting a penal orphanage and seeking specialist advice.

Dostoevsky in 1876

Meanwhile, the publication of the *Diary* month by month brought him nationwide fame.[100] Invitations flowed in to attend social occasions, meet with members of the Tsar's family, discuss spiritualism, give public readings and, in early 1878, to become a member of the Academy of Sciences. The increasing authority enjoyed by Dostoevsky's views was his passport to such celebrity. His epilepsy, though, did not change for the better while his emphysema obliged him to spend a month or so in Ems in the summer of 1876. The following year he turned his back on such treatment and spent the summer on the Kursk estate of Anna's brother. It was then that he took the opportunity to revisit his boyhood holiday home of Darovoe and the settlement of Chermashnia, featuring it in *The Brothers Karamazov*,[101] just as his adult holiday home of Staraya Russa became the Skotoprigonevsk of the novel's setting. The death of Nekrasov in 1877 reminded him how his career as a writer had begun with the generous reception given to *Poor Folk.* The *Diary* for December 1877 mentioned the fact in connection with the question of the differing assessments given to Nekrasov's poetry by the generations and immediately followed it with the announcement that the *Diary* would be abandoned for the time being in favour of a new work of fiction. Remembrance of things past allied to the issue of generational conflict brought into sharp focus the meaning of patricide as it was to be posed in *The Brothers Karamazov*.

The projected novel, while involving the murder of a father, was to be chiefly about justice, both human and divine. Three significant influences can be said to have been at work in its conception and execution. The most positive was that of Vladimir Solovev (1853–1900), Dostoevsky's close friend and ideological sympathizer, whose lectures on 'Godmanhood' he attended in 1878 when they electrified the St Petersburg intelligentsia and drew admiring crowds.[102] Both men shared the conviction that, once Europe had lost its religious vocation, humanity needed to reacquire a fundamental state of wholeness or all-unity (*vse-edinstvo*, as Solovev called it). Essential to such unity would be the example of Christ in a union between humanity and the world based on an identification not of God and man-become-God (in a Feuerbachian sense), but of a human–divine unity where belief in God and belief in man come together in the single full and complete truth of Godmanhood. Such an idea, however utopian, corresponded to Dostoevsky's thinking on the need to create a literal heaven-on-earth.

The second influence highlighted the heinous nature of the crime of patricide. It derived from the even more utopian thinking of a home-grown philosopher, N F Fedorov (pronounced F*yo*dorov, 1828–1903), author of *A Philosophy of the Common Cause* (*Filosofia obshchego dela*), who advocated the idea that it was the duty of humanity to direct its scientific energies to 'resurrection of the fathers', the literal resurrection of the dead. Dostoevsky had his attention directed to this idea by Fedorov's close disciple, N P Peterson, and discussed it enthusiastically with Solovev in March 1878.[103] The killing of a father could therefore be construed as directly contrary to the common cause of humanity.

The third influence related to the novel as a study in the miscarriage of justice, since it was based on the story of one of the 'unfortunates' Dostoevsky encountered in penal servitude, a certain Ilinsky who had been convicted of patricide but, as it later transpired, was innocent of the crime. The fate of Dmitry Karamazov obviously reflects this miscarriage. His trial scene, however, as described in the novel, is based on the famous political trial in March 1878 of Vera Zasulich, the terrorist accused of shooting the St Petersburg governor-general, Trepov. Dostoevsky attended the trial, consulted the lawyer A F Koni about trial procedure and even sympathized with the verdict of the jury when they acquitted her.[104] Simultaneously it introduced a political dimension into Dostoevsky's vision of his hero's future.

More important than the ideological aspect of the projected novel was its human relevance. Dostoevsky's fame as a writer had attracted attention from abroad and in April 1878 he was invited to attend an international congress in Paris scheduled for June, to be chaired by his hero, the French novelist Victor Hugo (1802–85). Aside from Dostoevsky's own poor health as an obstacle to foreign travel he was suddenly faced in May with the tragic

Father Ambrose the Starets of Optina Pustyn

death of his three-year-old son, Alesha, after a protracted epileptic attack. Conscious-stricken by the idea that the boy had died of his own disease, he found consolation a month later in a pilgrimage undertaken in Vladimir Solovev's company to the monastery of Optina Pustyn' in northern Russia. Here the famous monk Father Ambrose offered the novelist some words of comfort. It was upon him that Dostoevsky largely based the figure of the elder (*starets*) Zosima, portrayed in the novel as the spiritual father to his dead son's namesake, Alesha Karamazov. The visit to Optina Pustyn' thus provided the monastery setting and the novel's central ideas, elaborated and clarified in discussions with Solovev.

Throughout the summer Dostoevsky worked on the novel. Its gestation finally reached the point in November when he was ready to go to Moscow to discuss its publication in Katkov's *The Russian Messenger*. Satisfactory financial arrangements had already been made.[105] (By now he had paid most of his debts, even the 50 thalers he owed Turgenev.) The announcement that *The Brothers Karamazov* was due for publication in January 1879 quickly elicited invitations to attend St Petersburg literary salons and to give public readings. If attendance at the salons often bored him, the public readings were gladly accepted. Dostoevsky's popularity as a speaker, especially among the young, increased virtually in proportion to the amount of material from his new novel he was able to read in his charismatically thin, intense, spellbinding voice.

The Brothers Karamazov is a magnificent climax to Dostoevsky's career as a novelist. Although unfinished, it summarizes remarkably both his chief ideological concerns and his untiring interest in aberrant human psychology. To these are added a dimension of Christian commitment and spiritual meaning, graced by the 'soul of eternal memory',[106] that paradoxically turn a crime novel about the evils of lust and money into a profoundly philosophical and poetic debate about the *pro* and *contra* of moral choice. Though reality in the novel might be said to be confounded, even invaded on occasion, by the unreality of memory and dream, the main characters are not idea-figures; they emerge majestically from its pages in all their recognizably human verisimilitude and vulnerability. Its section headings and quasi-journalistic narration

View of Optina Pustyn

might give it a more than passing resemblance to the manner of *The Diary of a Writer*, but its fictional chronology, characterization and dramatic structure are inescapably redolent of the Dostoevskian novel at its most accomplished.

In four parts and an epilogue, *The Brothers Karamazov* is dedicated to Dostoevsky's wife, Anna, and designed to be the first of a two-part work. As the author notes in his preface: *The main novel is the second – the activity of my hero in our time, precisely at the present current moment. The first novel occurred 13 years ago and is scarcely even a novel, but only one moment from my hero's first youth.*[107]

His hero is Alesha, the youngest of the legitimate Karamazov brothers, whose destiny is to become a revolutionary. If the 'moment' from his first youth occurred 13 years before, then this might well refer to 1866 and the attempt by Karakozov to assassinate the Tsar. The political implication – in view of the Zasulich trial and the acts of terrorism perpetrated by the People's Will during the novel's composition – should not be overlooked. The 'moment', therefore, can be said to explain in part the idealism that turns Alesha into a revolutionary, though in terms of the novel's chronology it represents approximately only three days covering the events and ideological encounters of Parts I–III. Two months then elapse before the two-day trial of Part IV, followed by the brief epilogue. The most concentrated, chronologically, of all Dostoevsky's novels and the most confined in terms of setting, it centres in Parts I–III on exploring and exposing the truth of what happened before the miscarriage of justice that occurred at the trial. Who, then, murdered Fedor Pavlovich Karamazov and why?

The novel proceeds from the assumption that the trial of Dmitry – familiarly known as Mitia – Karamazov is an event of national importance. To this extent, the Karamazov family represents a cross-section of Russian ideological attitudes and attributes, a point clearly made at Mitia's trial when Ivan is said to rep-

A Karasin's illustration to *Brothers Karamazov*

resent European influences, Alesha 'the people's ideals' (*narodnye nachala*) and Mitia Russia as it was – though not the whole of it![108] The three brothers are the product of their father's two marriages: first to a wealthy, strong-willed woman who gave birth to Mitia; second, to a girl whose innocent little eyes, as he put it, *'slashed my soul like a razor'*,[109] who gave him Ivan and Alesha. Both his wives died and he was alleged to have fathered a further illegitimate son, Smerdiakov. The novel opens with a family gathering at the local monastery where the reprobate, sensual father (a magnificently robust portrayal of an elderly satyr) is to face mediation by the 65-year-old Father Zosima over his relations with his eldest son, Mitia, in the presence of Ivan and Alesha and other interested parties. The occasion raises issues that are pertinent to all subsequent events in the novel.

The rivalry between father and eldest son over the local beauty, Grushenka, for instance, or over money, although circumstantial in determining Mitia's guilt, comprises the '*external side*' of the novel, as the narrator puts it.[110] The 'true' or 'inner' story of what caused the ultimate tragic miscarriage of justice – which contributes to Zosima's readiness to fall on his knees in front of Mitia – begins with a discussion of state and church justice in the light of an article Ivan has recently published. His argument that the church should include the whole state (distantly echoing Solovev's theocratic thinking) ironically raises the issue of immortality and socialism. As is claimed, doubtless Ivan was merely amusing himself by not so much promoting the notion of church justice as destroying the idea of immortality on the principle that, if there is no immortality, there is no virtue (*dobro*) and consequently everything is permitted in the moral sphere.

Sensuality and love of life are features Dostoevsky particularly emphasizes in the portrayal of the Karamazovs. They may smell of crime (Rakitin's view), but theirs is a criminality of the senses, as it were, made explicit in Mitia's claim that beauty is a terrible

The road that inspired the *Brothers Karamazov*, Storoshil Staroi, near Moscow

and frightful thing because humanity can begin with the ideal of Madonna and end with the ideal of Sodom. He would have humanity made narrower. *'What is terrible is that beauty is not only frightful, but it is also mysterious. There God and the devil are at war and the battlefield is people's hearts.'*[111] In his relationships with both Grushenka and Katerina Ivanovna, whose evidence proves decisive at his trial, sensuality governs Mitia's actions. A driven man, elated ultimately to the point of ecstasy, he is in the end no more criminal than all sensual human insects.

The criminality resides with Ivan, the ostensibly Europeanized Russian and man of ideas. His meeting with his younger brother Alesha in the famous tavern scene (Book V) contains the most brilliant confessional writing Dostoevsky ever achieved. A self-confessed child of disbelief and doubt, nowhere did Dostoevsky project such disaffection more clearly than in Ivan Karamazov's essentially nihilistic attacks upon the notion of a just God and the idea of Christ as saviour of humanity. Ivan's Euclidean, earthy mind accepts the human need for God (even contending, as Voltaire observed, 'If God did not exist, it would be necessary to invent Him'), but he rebels against the world God has created since it offers scant evidence that, in the end, there will be a moment of eternal harmony in which all wickedness is forgiven. In the chapter 'Rebellion' (*Bunt*) Ivan offers, in his own Euclidean terms, horrific evidence of tortures meted out to the innocent, to children, and on that evidence he argues that God's world is not just; for, by implication, justice for the wicked cannot be seen to be done on earth and hell is no answer. So he will hand back his entrance ticket to God's world.

Alesha points out that Ivan has forgotten Christ. Ivan counters this charge with a projected poem entitled 'The Grand Inquisitor' (*Velikii inkvizitor*) in which he describes Christ returning to earth in Seville at the time of the Inquisition. Christ is arrested and confronted in prison by the 90-year-old Grand Inquisitor. What follows is a censure of Christ's teaching by the Grand Inquisitor, who all of his life has tried to love humanity, but has reached the conclusion that human beings are weak and rebellious.[112] Because Christ rejected the three temptations in the wilderness, summarized under the headings of mystery, miracle and authority, He has imposed upon humanity too great a burden of freedom of choice in the knowledge of good and evil. In the name of human happiness the Church (the Church of Rome in this case) has corrected Christ's teaching by using mystery, miracle and authority to suborn the human conscience, to offer, in short, the promise of immortality as a reward for earthly virtue. The Grand Inquisitor's view of humanity is essentially divisive in its assumption of a mass of people happy in the hope of everlasting life and an elect, the Church, that promises immortality, but knows there is nothing beyond the grave. Ever since its inception, the Church of Rome has been in league with the devil and is now in league with socialism. To all of this Christ the prisoner remains silent and responds finally by kissing the Grand Inquisitor on his bloodless lips.

One of the most plausible and awful indictments of Christianity, as Dostoevsky well knew, Christ's silence, though, like his kiss, is not intended to denote compliance. It presupposes the likelihood of eventual universal forgiveness. Alesha also kisses his brother when they part, but that is his sole instance of plagiarism since his response consists almost entirely of a hagiographic account of Father Zosima's sayings as recorded by him (Book VI, 'The Russian Monk' (*Russkii unok*)). Essentially, what Zosima wishes to teach is contained in what he says to his fellow monks on the morning of his final day: '*For you must know, my dearly beloved, that each single one of us is undoubtedly guilty for all and everything on earth, not only through a common worldly guilt, but each one individually for all people and for each person on this earth.*'[113] It is a message supported by his recollection of his older brother's insistence as he lay dying that *this* life is paradise and that immortality could mean Zosima living on for him as Alesha should live on for his mentor. Not a direct answer to Ivan's indictment, it presupposes that paradise is of the here and now and that, following the example of Job and Christ and the lesson of Zosima's own life, mutual responsibility for sin based on active love is a real guarantee of human harmony. Above all, it presupposes the importance of miracle.

The apportionment of guilt among the brothers Karamazov for the killing of their father is determined by sins of omission and commission. Ivan's is the greatest guilt because his nihilistically simplistic doctrine that everything is permitted in the moral sphere gives the lackey of his ideas, Smerdiakov, the justification for committing the deed. Precisely this fact is never divulged at the trial. All suspicion falls on Mitia who has issued murderous threats and finally claims Grushenka for himself. Arrested after a final orgy, he suffers the humiliation of being stripped naked before being charged. Smerdiakov has meanwhile obliquely confessed his guilt to an Ivan who, confronted by his personal devil in a *tour de force* of seedy impersonation, has to accept a satanic mockery of his ideas. Challenged finally to acknowledge the '*sanction of truth*', as his devilish guest puts it,[114] he throws a glass of water at him on the example of Luther's inkwell, knowing he can only save Mitia by performing an act of virtue.[115] Soon afterwards Ivan learns of Smerdiakov's suicide. It is now solely up to him to bear witness at the trial.

Crucial as his evidence is, he does no more than point to the money that Smerdiakov has stolen and claims ambiguously, in what to all appearances is a fit of insanity, that '*They all desire the death of the father. One beast will devour another.*'[116] This statement is incomprehensible to the court. Its nihilistic logic asserts the extremely egotistical wish to be free of all sanctions, particularly the sanction of biological fatherhood, let alone the sanction of the spiritual fatherhood of God. For Ivan the sanction of truth has become hopelessly compromised by his feverish mind's inability to tell the difference between the real and the fantastic. His mockery of spiritual truths is matched throughout the novel by more bizarre manifestations of the comically unreal than his own devil, such as the devils that supposedly appear in the monastery or Liza Khokhlakova's sado-masochistic dream of eating pineapple compote while watching a boy crucified to the back of a door.

In a work so complex, multifaceted and difficult to summarize, realism as a literary method is penetrated by the miraculous in many realistic ways. At Zosima's death, despite the shockingly rapid corruption of his body and Father Ferapont's imprecations, Alesha, the realist-believer, sees his mentor come to him from among the guests of Christ's first miracle in Cana of Galilee. In one of the greatest passages in all literature he then goes out into the monastery garden and flings himself on the ground beneath the starry sky:

O, he wept in his delight even at these stars which shone at him from infinity and 'he was not ashamed of this ecstasy'. It was as if threads from all these numberless worlds God had created entered his soul at that moment and his soul quivered 'in its contact with other worlds'. He wanted to forgive everyone for everything and to ask forgiveness – O, not for himself! – for all people, for all and everything. 'They will then ask forgiveness for me!' rang out in his soul. But with each moment he felt lucidly and consciously that something firm and unshakeable as the heavens above him had entered his soul. Some idea or other had taken command of his mind and would be there all his life and forever. He had fallen on the earth a weak youth and had risen up a firm fighter for the rest of his life and knew and felt this all of a sudden at the very moment of his ecstasy. And never in all his life would Alesha forget this moment. 'Someone visited my soul at that instant,' he would say afterwards with firm belief in his own words.[119]

The final words of the novel rest with him. When he speaks to his boy disciples at the grave of Iliusha on the eve of his departure from the monastery, he proclaims the irreplaceable value of memory, especially from childhood, and the miraculous reality of eternal life. Yes, we will all rise again and see each other and joyfully tell each other about the past, is his response to Kolia Krasotkin's question. The subtext of *The Brothers Karamazov* hints at the need for reconciliation between the generations, for the psychic transformation of mankind, for resurrection as a reality and mutual responsibility for sin based on active love as the sole source of world harmony.

Alesha and Ilyushechka from the *Brothers Karamazov* an illustration by Lodyagin, 1955

Final Triumph

Although *The Brothers Karamazov* was not completed until December 1880, it had attracted enormous interest since it began its uneven publication almost two years previously. Struggling throughout from ill health and epileptic seizures, with a visit to Bad Ems in the summer of 1879 for treatment of his emphysema, Dostoevsky had enhanced his reputation with this novel even more than with his *Diary*. He now clearly enjoyed an ascendancy over his rival, Turgenev, when the latter made a triumphant return from his chosen Paris exile in the same year. Their joint public readings on behalf of the Literary Fund demonstrated Dostoevsky's evident success, even if his pro-Tsarist attitude contrasted with Turgenev's implied support for a constitution. Despite his pro-Tsarist sympathies, as an ex-convict Dostoevsky was still being observed by the secret police. Only after the apparent intervention of Grand Duke Constantine, the Tsar's brother and an admirer of his, was he free of such surveillance.

Then came the moment of his greatest triumph. It provided a final contrast between his ultra-nationalist sympathies and the Eurocentric ideals of his rival. At the height of the period known as 'the dictatorship of the heart', when Loris-Melikov had been appointed by the Tsar to stem the increasing wave of terrorist activity by the People's Will, an event of great national and cultural importance occurred in Moscow in June 1880: the unveiling of a statue of Alexander Pushkin, Russia's greatest poet. Greatest, though, in what sense? This question needed a clear answer and Turgenev and Dostoevsky, as Russia's most illustrious writers (Tolstoy refused to attend), were expected to give it.

The celebrations at the unveiling lasted for two days. Turgenev spoke on the first day and could not bring himself to declare unequivocally that Pushkin was a great national poet. He heaped praise on the poet's reputation and achievement, but concluded on what may have seemed a slightly defensive note by hoping that a future admirer of the statue would acknowledge to himself that he had become more Russian, more educated and more free as a man through Pushkin's poetry. 'In poetry,' concluded Turgenev, 'there is a liberating, because ennobling, moral force', and that is what Pushkin could teach the Russian people.[118]

Dostoevsky's much longer address the following day was unequivocal. It opened with the well-known assessment by Gogol that 'Pushkin is an extraordinary phenomenon and perhaps a unique manifestation of the Russian spirit,'[119] to which Dostoevsky significantly added: *And prophetic.*[120] This claim elicited immediate cries of approval. The tone was set for what became the greatest triumph of his career, in which respect and admiration for his own achievement matched his own insightful and idiosyncratic appraisal of Pushkin's place in Russian culture. Despite occasionally bordering on the grandiose in its rhetorical manner, the address is carefully focused on Pushkin's work, claiming, for example, a threefold pattern in the poet's career that

Puskin the bard of the Russian Empire

ranges from the type of 'homeless wanderer' exemplified by Aleko (of 'The Gypsies') and Onegin, to the ultimate accolade of Pushkin as a figure of world significance. The second phase of Pushkin's career culminated in Onegin's rejection by Tatiana in what was an extremely valuable examination of the dilemma that led Dostoevsky to proclaim him *a great national writer, unlike anyone before him.*[121] The third phase, however, saw him as a national genius capable of incarnating the genius of all other nations. Although a claim of implausible magnitude, it chimed with Dostoevsky's ideal of world harmony and formed part of a concluding vision of Russia's destiny that was not so much national as supranational or, as one sentence expressed it: *I am only speaking of the brotherhood of people and of the fact that the Russian heart, perhaps, of all national hearts is the most attuned to an idea of global, all-human fraternal unity, and I see traces of this in our history, in our most gifted men and women and in the artistic genius of Pushkin.*[122]

Dostoevsky in 1879

This was the prophetic essence of Pushkin's genius as Dostoevsky saw it. No doubt it was part of the great secret that the poet took to his premature grave. At a time when Russia was beset by terrorism, its intelligentsia riven more than ever by factions, Dostoevsky's intensely patriotic vision of the national destiny met a deeply felt need for reassurance. It was also prophetic for Dostoevsky. His estimate of Pushkin's greatness, however far-fetched and challenged though it was,[123] implied a similar global and supranational fame for himself.

Dostoevsky said more than once that he had work planned for another 20 years, but he also complained of failing health and witnesses to his final days mention his increasingly sickly appearance. The final months of 1880 were taken up with a renewal of his *The Diary of a Writer*, in which among other articles he published his Pushkin address. He became preoccupied in print with the relations between Russia and Asia. At no time did he appear to make detailed plans to write the second part of his final novel and his last known notebook is chiefly given over to jottings about the Russian economy and finances. Among them, of course, was the famous self-estimate: *They call me a psychologist: it's not true, I am merely a realist in a higher sense, that is to say I describe all the depths of the human soul.*[124]

This insight is made all the more profound by Dostoevsky's approaching death. Until late January 1881 there was little sign of immediate danger to his health, but during the night of 25–6 January, after a pleasant family dinner at which he had spoken excitedly of his admiration for Charles Dickens and *The Pickwick Papers* (1836–7), he suffered a nosebleed. The next day his condition worsened.[125] A doctor and specialist attended in quick succession and Dostoevsky was given the last rites, but the flow of blood from his mouth was staunched for a time and on the 27th there were hopes for some improvement. When he woke the next morning, though, he told Anna he would die that day and his intuition was accurate. After falling into a coma from a further haemorrhage, he died at about 8.30 p.m. on 28 January 1881. At his death, as if in manifest proof of his own hopes for world harmony, all the diverse factions in Russian society united temporarily to mourn his passing and pay their respects to his memory.

The Tsar granted Anna a pension, the first such award ever

Anna, Liuba and Fedya at Dostoevsky's Graveside 1881

made to an author's widow. At the funeral on 31 January Dostoevsky's coffin was followed by a procession of thousands through the streets of St Petersburg to its final resting place in the Alexander Nevsky Lavra, where the interment occurred on 1 February. Tributes were paid to his martyr's life, but most touching of all were Vladimir Solovev's words. He hoped that Dostoevsky's love for the living human soul, for its infinite strength that could overcome all adversity, would contribute to the reconciliation of all Russians.

Dostoevsky took the secret of world harmony to his grave. Two months after his funeral, on 1 March 1881, Tsar Alexander II was assassinated by a bomb-thrower of the People's Will. The vision of a united people reconciled by love proved the least viable of Dostoevsky's ideals. With its history of revolution, civil war, party dictatorship and ideological tyranny, Russia in the twentieth century mirrored more exactly the dysfunctional, unregenerate world he projected in his fiction. If he never properly appreciated the true meaning of freedom as a political ideal, despite his own sufferings, Dostoevsky never flinched from engaging with its meaning in moral terms and holding fast to the need for faith in a moral context. Yet all of his life he was a self-confessed doubter. This paradox lies at the heart of his appeal.

Dostoevsky confronted the reader with powerful novels that bear the hallmark of tragedy, but in essence are explorations of the psychological dilemma posed by motives *pro* and *contra*. The most accessible and popular of his novels has always been *Crime and Punishment* and its hero, Raskolnikov, who has to live out the consequences of his dialectics. Similarly, few images in literature have been more attractive than that of the Christ-like idiot Prince Myshkin who hopes to change the world with his message of a transforming beauty. No more devilish and prophetic picture of a world possessed by nihilism or various shades of fanaticism, political and otherwise, appears in nineteenth-century literature than *The Devils*, while *The Brothers Karamazov* raises the crime novel to the level of profound philosophical debate in its dialectical examination of the nature of justice.

Dostoevsky's funeral procession by Baldinger, 1881

Out of origins in Romanticism and Gothic horror Dostoevsky created monumental and realistic works that have a polymathic as well as polyphonic range, but mix the realistic with the fantastic,

Dostoevsky's memorial in the Alexander Nevsky Lavra, St Petersburg

the ideal with the evil, the supposedly fixed norms of the rational with the realities of nightmare. The Dostoevskian novel has come to be regarded as the most original and influential of the literary legacies bequeathed by the nineteenth century and yet his own life can rival his literary reputation in its unique record of personal misfortune matched by ultimate renown, epilepsy and weak health compounded by seemingly endless financial worries and, finally, years of unsatisfactory relationships crowned by the miraculous happiness of a devoted young wife and a loving family.

Dostoevsky was a nineteenth-century Everyman. In his sensuality, contentiousness, mockery and arrogance he was all too human. In his deep compassion for 'the insulted and injured', his spirituality, humour and erudition he was touched by sainthood. His brilliant powers of expression brought alive his age. Even if his novels can seem long-winded and arduous to read by modern standards, when read with understanding they have the power to ambush a part of life and transform it for ever.

Notes

1. Letter to V P Gorchakov, 1822.
2. First demonstrated by R I Ivanov-Razumnik in his *Pushkin i Belinskii* (Petrograd, 1916).
3. Dates in nineteenth-century Russia were 12 days behind those in the West and are designated by O S (i.e. Old Style). All dates in the text are O S unless otherwise indicated.
4. *F M Dostoevskii, Polnoe sobranie sochinenii v tridtsati tomakh,* Tom. XXII, L., 1981, 49. All future references to this source, the definitive edition of Dostoevsky's works in 30 volumes, will refer to *PSS,* followed by the volume and page numbers.
5. This novel, the least successful of his major works, has also been translated as *A Raw Youth* (Constance Garnett) and *The Adolescent* (Andrew R MacAndrew).
6. Letter of 9 August 1838; *PSS*, 28, bk 1, 50.
7. *PSS*, 28, bk 1, 53–4.
8. Sigmund Freud, 'Dostoevsky and Parricide,' in *Collected Works*, Vol. XIV (Frankfurt, 1968), pp. 399–418.
9. The fullest examination of Dostoevsky and epilepsy is to be found in James L Rice, *Dostoevsky and the Healing Art: An Essay in Literary and Medical History* (Ardis, Ann Arbor, 1985).
10. *PSS*, 28, bk 1, 63.
11. When first published in 1861 it was unsigned and thought to be attributable to a contributor to the journal, D D Minaev, but according to his friend N N Strakhov, Dostoevsky himself wrote the feuilleton entitled 'St Petersburg Dreams Visions in Verse and Prose'. This passage is borrowed in part from the ending to his short story 'A Weak Heart' ('Slaboe serdtse', 1848) and anticipates Raskolnikov's mesmerized contemplation of the Neva after having committed murder in *Crime and Punishment*.
12. *PSS*, 19, 68–9.
13. *PSS*, 25, 30.

14 *PSS*, 25, 31.

15 V. Kirpotin, *Dostoevskii i Belinskii*, izd. vtoroe, M., 1976, p. 299.

16 See *PSS* 28, bk.1, 224.

17 The most recent study of Speshnev's life and influence is to be found in Liudmila Saraskina's *Fedor Dostoevskii. Odolenie demonov* (Moscow, 1996).

18 Mikhail Bakhtin first published his famous *Problems of Dostoevsky's Art* in 1929. Because his ideas did not exactly meet the relatively simplistic requirements of a dogmatic Socialist Realism, his work was not republished until 1963. It appeared in an enlarged form as *Problems of Dostoevsky's Poetics* after he had spent several decades in enforced exile in Kazakhstan. His views became well known in the West during the 1970s and 1980s due to the work principally of American scholars. He is most famous for his argument that Dostoevsky's novels (though he in fact never analysed one of the novels in depth) are characterized by (his italics) '*A plurality of independent and unmerged voices and consciousnesses, a genuine polyphony of fully valid voices* . . . Dostoevsky's major heroes are, by the very nature of his creative design, *not only objects of authorial discourse but also subjects of their own directly signifying discourse*' (*Problems of Dostoevsky's Poetics*, ed. and trans. by Caryl Emerson (Manchester University Press, 1984), pp. 6–7). Polyphony as such is arguably not a method exclusive to Dostoevsky; and its use as a term of approval by comparison with the use of 'monological' in reference, say, to Tolstoy seems wilfully perverse.

19 *PSS,* 2, 295.

20 *PSS*, 28, bk 1, 164.

21 See Geir Kjetsaa, *Dostoevsky and his New Testament* (Solum Forlag/Humanities Press, New Jersey, 1984), for a scholarly description and examination of the actual copy.

22 *PSS*, 4, 98.

23 *PSS*, 28, bk 1, 177.

24 *PSS*, 28, bk 1, 176.

25 A E Vrangel', '*Iz "Vospominanii o F M Dostevskom v Sibiri", F M Dostoevskii v vospomianiakh sovremennikov*, Vol. I, 1964, 251. It is chiefly from these memoirs that we know about Dostoevsky's life in Semipalatinsk.

26 *PSS*, 2, 336.

27 The term refers to 'different ranks', i.e. the 14-rank hierarchy established by Peter the Great in the eighteenth century. For an examination of its origins see Lindsey Hughes, *Russia in the Age of Peter the Great* (Yale University Press, 2000), pp 180–5.

28 See Turgenev's lecture *Gamlet i Don Kikhot*, 1860.

29 For an extended examination of these ideas, see volume 3 of Joseph Frank's definitive biography *Dostoevsky: The Stir of Liberation* (Princeton University Press, 1986).

30 See especially Andrzej Walicki, *The Slavophile Controversy* (Oxford University Press, 1975).

31 *PSS*, 3, 208.

32 *PPS*, 3, 386.

33 *PSS*, 3, 245.

34 *PSS*, 5, 93.

35 *PSS*, 5, 72.

36 *Voprosy literatury*, 7 (1957), 132.

37 Her sister, Nadezhda, was to become famous as Russia's first woman doctor and Polina herself was later to marry V V Rozanov, one of Dostoevsky's most celebrated pre-revolutionary commentators.

38 In fact, *podpol'e* (gen. *podpol'ia*) does not mean 'underground' so much as 'semi-basement', the area below-stairs.

39 *PSS*, 5, 99.

40 Joseph Frank, in his elaborate but sensitive and deeply probing interpretation of this work, has described it as 'a brilliantly Swiftian satire' (*The Stir of Liberation*, 1986, p 316), but no disrespect is intended if it is made clear that it is no *Gulliver's Travels*.

41 *PSS*, 5, 119. I have added the 'bloodies' to emphasize the Underground Man's bloody-mindedness and offer my apologies to Dostoevsky for this much translator's licence. [RF]

42 *PSS*, 28, bk 1, 176.

43 *PSS*, 20, 174–5.

44 *PSS*, 5, 179.

45 *PSS*, 28, bk 2, 116.

46 *PSS*, 28, bk 2, 136–7.

47 See *The Notebooks for Crime and Punishment*, ed. and trans. by

Edward Wasiolek (Chicago University Press, 1967). Volume 7 of the definitive edition of Dostoevsky's works (*'Nauka',* Leningrad, 1973) contains all the original manuscript notes for the novel, as well as copious and extremely useful annotation. Their survival demonstrates the care taken by Dostoevsky and the problems he encountered during the novel's composition.

48 This aspect of the form of the novel was first studied by Viacheslav Ivanov (*Borozdy i mezhi*, Moscow, 1916). To him we also owe the description of the Dostoevskian novel as a novel-tragedy (*roman-tragediia*). Konstantin Mochulsky developed the notion further in his famous study first published in 1947 (*Dostoevskii*, Paris) and translated in 1967 (*Dostoevsky*, trans. Michael A. Minihan, Princeton, New Jersey). Mochulsky paid particular attention to the construction of the Dostoevskian novel and the role of sub-plots.

49 *PSS,* 6, 422.

50 *PSS*, 6, 54.

51 Some commentators have referred to a 'narrator' in *Crime and Punishment*. There is no such identifiable component in the fiction and the use of the term is an unnecessary mystification.

52 *PSS*, 6, 63.

53 Strictly speaking, this was not a new idea in Dostoevsky's work. The notion that humanity could be divided into dominant and dominated is present in the Underground Man's confession and easily identifiable in his first work *Poor Folk*, in the contrast between Devushkin (from *devushka*: 'a girl') and Bykov (from *Byk*: 'a bull'), his rival and victor. Several other sources for the idea have been suggested, such as G W F Hegel's *Philosophy of History* (1817), Honoré de Balzac's *Le Père Goriot* (1834), Nikolai Chernyshevsky's 'new men', references in Pushkin and Pisarev, and a work by Napoleon III on Julius Caesar published in 1865, but equally plausible and apposite as source for the Napoleonic theme could be the arrogant self-aggrandizement of Bazarov in Turgenev's *Fathers and Sons*. For a discussion of some of these issues see Joseph Frank's *Dostoevsky: The Miraculous Years, 1865–1871* (Princeton University Press, 1995), pp 68–79.

54 *PSS*, 6, 199.

55 *PSS*, 6, 202.
56 *PSS*, 6, 322.
57 *PSS*, 6, 419.
58 Henry James offered this verdict in a letter to Hugh Walpole dated 19 May 1912.
59 The name 'Astley' was apparently taken from Elizabeth Gaskell's novel, *Ruth* (1853).
60 *PSS*, 28, bk 2, 210.
61 *PSS*, 28, bk 2, 211.
62 'It is not at all implausible . . . to imagine that Prince Myshkin's attempt to live by the highest Christian values in the modern world . . . is linked in some subconscious fashion with Dostoevsky's struggles to tell the truth about "My Acquaintance with Belinsky".' *Dostoevsky. The Miraculous Years, 1865–1871* (Princeton University Press, 1995), p 230. Dostoevsky's article was never published, nor has any copy been traced.
63 It is not known how Dostoevsky met Ogarev (pronounced 'Oga*ryo*v') in Geneva, but he had probably first met him in London in 1862 when he visited Herzen. Ogarev (1813–77) was Herzen's close friend and collaborator. A talented poet, he was of such an easy-going nature that he even allowed Herzen to cuckold him with his second wife, though by the time he had moved to Geneva he had lost most of his money and was living with an English prostitute, Mary Sutherland. She eventually brought him to the London suburb of Greenwich where he died.
64 *PSS*, 28, bk 2, 240–1.
65 *PSS*, 28, bk 2, 251.
66 Few things were more idiotic at this point in his life than the appearance of a strange work by Paul Grimm entitled *Les Mystères du Palais des Czars sous l'Empereur Nicolas I* (Wurzburg, 1868). Set in 1855, it told of a certain Theodore Dostoiewsky's return from Siberia, his part in a revolutionary conspiracy, his arrest, refusal to betray comrades, his sentence to a flogging and Siberia and death *en route* despite a last-minute pardon. Nicholas I ends by poisoning himself. Dostoevsky considered making an official protest and even drafted a letter (see *PSS*, 28, bk 2, 315), but then let the matter drop.

67 *PSS*, 28, bk 2, 277.

68 *PSS*, 28, bk 2, 297.

69 *PSS*, 8, 351.

70 Composed in 1829, the poem was first published in Pushkin's own journal *The Contemporary* in 1837.

71 *PSS*, 8, 380.

72 *PSS*, 8, 195.

73 *PSS*, 8, 339.

74 *PSS*, 8, 344.

75 *PSS*, 8, 510.

76 These notes have survived (see *PSS*, 9, 125–39 and 499–524), but it requires some very imaginative guesswork to elicit sense from them and to suggest that they are coherent is frankly unwise. Certain features and names (e.g. Tikhon, Lambert, etc.) evidently point to plotlines and characters in *The Devils*, *An Accidental Family* (*Podrostok*) and *The Brothers Karamazov* (*Brat'ia Karamazovy*).

77 Dostoevsky is supposed to have based the story partly on his friend Baron Wrangel's affair with Mme Gerngross, the sexually active wife of the general commanding the garrison in Semipalatinsk between 1856 and 1858.

78 *PSS*, 29, bk 1, 141.

79 Joseph Frank, for example, dismisses Anna's – Dostoevsky's wife's – account in her memoirs that news about Ivanov prompted Dostoevsky to begin a novel with Ivanov as hero (see Frank, *The Miraculous Years* (1995), p 396). Fear of perlustration, especially in letters to his publisher, must have made Dostoevsky cautious.

80 Kraevsky was owner and editor of a leading 'fat journal' *Fatherland Notes* (*Otechesvennye zapiski*) for which Belinsky worked as literary critic in the 1840s, but it was unfair of Dostoevsky to lump them together in this way. Kraevsky, a hard-nosed and exploitative employer, eventually became Belinsky's sworn enemy.

81 The brothers Serno-Solovevich, Alexander (1838–69) and Nikolai (*d.* 1866), were notable as members of the revolutionary movement of the 1860s and associates of Chernyshevsky.

82 *PSS*, 29, bk 1,145.

83 *PSS,* 10, 24.

84 A special ironic pretentiousness is attached to Stavrogin's name as to others. Arguably based on *stavros* (i.e.'a cross'), the name might mean someone who has a cross to bear (partly explained by his *Confession* in the unpublished chapter 'At Tikhon's'). Other names have faintly parodic meanings: Verkhovensky suggests 'heights', i.e. of authority, nobility, even princeliness; Shatov intimates 'shakiness'; Kirillov, saintliness, e.g. St Cyril; others suggested birds – Drozdov from *drozd* ('thrush'), Lebiadkin from *lebed* ('swan'), Skvoreshniki from *skvorechnik* ('starling-house'), etc. Karmazinov evokes the name of Karamzin (1766–1826), famous as Russia's first historian and the author of a classically famous work of Sentimentalism, *Poor Liza* (*Bednaia Liza*, 1792). Associations with the Book of Revelations have also been identified by several recent commentators.

85 *PSS*, 10, 94.

86 *PSS*, 10, 187–8.

87 *PSS*, 10, 469.

88 *PSS*, 10, 198.

89 *PSS*, 10, 299.

90 *PSS*, 10, 372–3.

91 *PSS*, 10, 506.

92 Dostoevsky based his vision of a Golden Age on a picture by Claude Lorrain, 'Acis and Galatea', which he greatly admired in the Dresden art gallery.

93 *PSS*, 11, 21–2.

94 The passage on genre devoted to *Bobok* in Mikhail Bakhtin's *Problems of Dostoevsky's Poetics* is among the most valuable in his study of Dostoevsky's use of Menippean satire, though not every reader would agree with the claim that 'We would hardly be mistaken in saying that "Bobok", in all its depth and boldness, is one of the greatest menippea in all world literature' (trans. Emerson, p. 138).

95 Vs S Solovev, *F M Dostoevskii v vospominanii sovremennikov*, Vol. II, *izd. 'Khudozh. lit'*, 1964, 189. Vsevolod Solovev (pron. Solov*yov*) was the elder brother of the philosopher Vladimir who was later to become Dostoevsky's close friend.

96 This title was used for my translation of the novel (World's

Classics, 1994) on the grounds that *A Raw Youth* or *The Adolescent* was hardly a satisfactory description by modern standards of the narrator, a 20-year-old writing about his 19-year-old self.

97 In the case of a girl who committed suicide, Olia, her mother's name changes inexplicably from Daria Onisimovna to Nastasia Yegorovna in the course of the novel.

98 *PSS*, 13, 311.

99 *PSS*, 13, 455.

100 During 1876–7 the initial print run was 2,000 copies, which increased to 3,000, then to 4,000 in summer (with July–August combined due to Dostoevsky's absence) and 6,000 in winter months.

101 The transliterated title is *Brat'ia Karamazovy* and can be translated as either *The Brothers Karamazov* or *The Karamazov Brothers*. I have preferred to retain the Russian word order. The meaning of the name has been variously interpreted, but in the novel it is interpreted by Snegirev's mad wife as 'those who are painted black'. 'Guilt-daubed' is Richard Peace's suggestion in his excellent *Dostoyevsky: An Examination of the Major Novels* (Cambridge University Press, 1971), pp 281–2. For detailed commentaries on the novel see Victor Terras, *A Karamazov Companion* (Wisconsin University Press, 1981) and the fifth and final volume of Joseph Frank's monumental biography, *The Mantle of the Prophet* (Princeton University Press/Robson, 2002, pp 567–703).

102 At one such lecture Dostoevsky met his friend Strakhov, who appeared oddly evasive. He had accompanied Tolstoy to the lecture, but the latter wished to remain incognito. Dostoevsky regretted that there had been no meeting and in fact the two writers never met.

103 *PSS*, 30, bk 1, letter 734.

104 Trial by jury in criminal cases was a relatively new phenomenon in Russia, introduced among the reforms instituted in the 1860s in the wake of the liberation of the serfs and still a contentious issue in the late 1870s. Vera Zasulich (1849–1919), incensed by a flogging administered to a student on Trepov's orders for failing to remove his cap in deference, was no dedicated terrorist, although her shooting of Trepov in the pelvis helped to initiate the period

of terrorism of the People's Will. She subsequently became a Marxist. See Jay Bergman, *Vera Zasulich* (Stanford University Press, 1983).

105 Diane Oenning Thompson has expressed this admirably: 'In *The Brothers Karamazov*, the soul of eternal memory receives its most condensed expression in the Epigraph where Christ prophecies two possibilities: if the corn of wheat does not fall to earth and die, "it abideth alone"; if it does, then "it bringeth forth much fruit". On this opposition the novel's dramatic enactment of the *pro* and *contra* was formed. [. . .] Thus the whole novel enacts a progressive metaphorical fulfilment of the Epigraph' (*The Brothers Karamazov and the Poetics of Memory* (Cambridge University Press, 1991), p 324).

106 *PSS*, 14, 6.

107 L Grossman, *Dostoevskii*, izd. *'Molodaia gvardiia'* (Moscow, 1965), pp 569–71.

108 *PSS*, 15, 128.

109 *PSS*, 14, 13.

110 *PSS*, 14, 12.

111 *PSS*, 14,100.

112 In a brief introduction to his public reading of the chapter on 30 December 1879, Dostoevsky was supposed to have claimed that his Grand Inquisitor is an atheist and the point of the chapter is *if you distort Christian faith by linking it to the aims of this world the whole sense of Christianity is instantly lost, the intellect must undoubtedly collapse into disbelief and instead of the great Christian ideal all that is created is a new Tower of Babel* [. . .] *and under the guise of* social *love of humanity there will emerge blatant contempt for it* (*PSS*, 15, 198).

113 *PSS*, 14, 159.

114 *PSS*, 15, 84.

115 Martin Luther (1483–1546) apparently saw the devil and threw an inkwell at him.

116 *PSS*, 15, 117.

117 *PSS*, 14, 328.

118 I S Turgenev, *Polnoe sobranie sochinenii i pisem*, XV (M-L, 1968), p 76.

119 From Gogol's article on Pushkin in *Arabesques* (1835), to which he

added: 'He is a Russian man in his development, as perhaps he will appear to be in 200 years time.'

120 *PSS*, 26, 136.

121 *PSS*, 26, 143.

122 *PSS*, 26, 148.

123 The challenge by Leontiev, for example, is interestingly examined in Chapter 30 of Joseph Franks's fifth volume.

124 *PSS*, 27, 65.

125 It is possible that on the night of the 25th Dostoevsky may have been disturbed by a police search in an adjacent apartment occupied by A I Barannikov. Barannikov, a member of the People's Will, had been the accomplice of Kravchinsky (known as 'Stepniak') who achieved fame for killing General Mezentsev, the St Petersburg chief of police, in broad daylight in 1878. 'Stepniak' escaped arrest and eventually emigrated to England, wrote several books, enjoyed renown as a spokesman for Russian freedom and died after being run over by a train near his home in Bedford Park, London, shortly before Christmas 1895.

Chronology

Year	Age	Life
1821		Born 30 October to Mikhail and Maria Dostoevsky in the Hospital for the Poor, Moscow, where his father was a doctor.
1833–7	12–15	At school in Moscow.
1837		Mother dies 27 February. In May he and brother Mikhail are sent to St Petersburg to enter Engineering Academy.
1838	16	16 January he enters Engineering Academy. Mikhail sent to Tallinn.
1839	17	8 June father dies in mysterious circumstances.
1840–1	19–20	Works on historical dramas related to Mary Stuart and Boris Godunov.
1841		5 August obtains officer rank.
1843	21	12 August completes engineering course and is enrolled in Engineering Corps.
1844	22	June–July his translation of Balzac's *Eugénie Grandet* published. 19 October obtains discharge from military service. Devotes himself to writing.
1845	23	Completes first work *Poor Folk*. Friendship with Belinsky.
1846	24	January, publication of *Poor Folk*. In February, *The Double*.
1847	26	Break with Belinsky. He begins visiting the Petrashevsky meetings. October–December, *The Landlady* published.
1848	27	*A Weak Heart* and *White Nights* published.

Year	History	Culture
1821	Famine in Ireland.	Thomas De Quincey, *Confessions of an English Opium-Eater.* Hegel, *Philosophy of Right.*
1833	In British Empire, slavery abolished. Michael Faraday discovers electrolysis.	Felix Mendelssohn, *Fourth Symphony.*
1837	In Britain, William IV dies; Victoria becomes queen (until 1901). In US, Martin van Buren becomes president.	Charles Dickens, *Pickwick Papers.*
1838	In Britain, People's Charter initiates Chartist movement.	In London, National Gallery opens.
1839	Treaty of London: Belgium's independence guaranteed.	Chopin, *Twenty-four Preludes.* M Y Lermontov, *A Hero of Our Time.*
1840	In New Zealand, Treaty of Waitangi: Maori chiefs surrender sovereignty to Britain.	Robert Schumann, *Dichterliebe* Adolphe Sax invents the saxophone.
1841	In east Africa, Said ibn Sayyid makes Zanzibar his capital.	In Britain, Punch magazine founded.
1843	In India, Britain annexes Sind. In south Africa, Britain proclaims Natal a colony.	Donizetti, *Don Pasquale.* Wagner, *Flying Dutchman.* Dickens, *A Christmas Carol.*
1844	In Morocco, war with France.	Alexandre Dumas, *The Count of Monte Cristo.* Søren Aabye Kierkegaard, *The Concept of Dread.*
1845	In Ireland, potato famine. In India, Anglo-Sikh War (until 1848-9).	Friedrich Engels, *The Condition of the Working Classes in England.*
1846	Mexico-US War (until 1848). In southern Africa, second Xhosa War.	Hector Berlioz, *The Damnation of Faust.*
1847	In Yucután Peninsula, War of the Castes. In France, reform banquets held. In Switzerland, Sonderbund War.	Verdi, *Macbeth.* Charlotte Brontë, *Jane Eyre.* Emily Brontë, *Wuthering Heights.*
1848	In continental Europe, revolutions in: Sicily; Naples; Paris; Vienna; Venice; Milan; Warsaw; and Cracow. In France, Second Republic begins (until 1851). Treaty of Guadeloupe: US authority over western and south-western states.	Elizabeth Gaskell, *Mary Barton.* William Thackeray, *Vanity Fair.* Engels and Karl Marx, *The Communist Manifesto.* Mill, *Principles of Political Economy.*

Year	Age	Life
1849	28	*Netochka Nezvanova* published. Associates with Palm-Durov circle. 15 April reads aloud Belinsky's *Letter to Gogol* at Petrashevsky meeting. 23 April arrested and imprisoned in the Alekseevsky Ravelin of the Peter and Paul Fortress. April–November investigated and tried. 22 December mock execution; sentence commuted to 4 years hard labour followed by service in the ranks.
1850		Arrives at Omsk penal settlement.
1854	32	February, release from penal servitude. Transferred to Semipalatinsk for military service in the ranks. Friendship with Baron Wrangel.
1856	34	Petitions for reinstatement of rights. 1 October obtains officer status.
1857	35	6 February first marriage to Marsha Isaeva.
1859	37	Publication of *Uncle's Dream* and *The Village of Stepanchikovo*. Obtains release from Siberian exile. Returns to European Russia, first to Tver and, in December, to St Petersburg.
1860	38–9	Publication of first parts of *The House of the Dead*. First 2-vol. edition of his works published in Moscow.
1861	40	With his brother starts publishing the journal *Time*. Publishes his novel *The Insulted and Injured* in *Time* and completes publication of *The House of the Dead*.
1862		First journey abroad. Visits Berlin, Paris, London (Crystal Palace) and Florence. Infatuated with Polina Suslova.
1863	42	Publishes *Winter Notes of Summer Impressions* in *Time*. 24 May journal banned by government decree. Second trip abroad. Begins gambling. Mad about Suslova.
1864	43	Mikhail receives permission to publish new journal *Epoch*. 16 May death of Marsha. 10 July death of Mikhail. Publishes *Notes from the Underground* in *Epoch*.
1865	44	June *Epoch* fails. Incurs serious debts. Goes abroad, gambles and becomes stranded in Wiesbaden. Begins *Crime and Punishment*.
1866	45	*Crime and Punishment* published. Engages stenographer Anna Snitkina to write *The Gambler*.

Year	History	Culture
1849	In Rome, republic proclaimed; French troops take Rome. In India, Britain annexes Punjab.	Dickens, *David Copperfield.*
1850	In Rome, Pope Pius IX restored.	Nathaniel Hawthorne, *The Scarlet Letter.* Lord Tennyson, *In Memoriam.*
1854	In US, Republican Party founded.	Hector Berlioz, *The Childhood of Christ.*
1856	In India, Britain annexes Oudh. Treaty of Paris: integrity of Turkey is recognized.	
1857	In India, mutiny against the British (until 1858).	Charles Baudelaire, *Les Fleurs du Mal.* Gustave Flaubert, *Madame Bovary.*
1859	Franco-Piedmontese War against Austria. Spanish-Moroccan War (until 1860). Construction of Suez Canal begins (until 1869).	C F Gounod, *Faust.* Wagner, *Tristan und Isolde.* George Eliot, *Adam Bede.* Edouard Manet, *Absinthe Drinker.*
1860	In Italy, unification achieved by invasions of Garibaldi and Victor Emmanuel respectively. In New Zealand, Taranaki wars.	Ivan Turgenev, *On the Eve.* George Eliot, *The Mill on the Floss.*
1861	In US, Abraham Lincoln becomes president (until 1865). In US, Civil War begins (until 1865). In Russia, serfdom abolished.	Dickens, *Great Expectations.* Eliot, *Silas Marner.* In Britain, William Morris begins to make wallpapers and tapestries.
1862	In Prussia, Otto von Bismarck becomes premier.	Turgenev, *Fathers and Sons.* Verdi, *La Forza del Destino.* Hugo, *Les Misérables.*
1863	In US, slavery abolished. In Asia, Cambodia becomes French protectorate. Polish uprising against Russia.	Berlioz, *The Trojans (part I).* Charles Kingsley, *The Water Babies.* Ernest Renan, *La vie de Jésus.* Manet, *Déjeuner sur l'herbe.*
1864	In London, Karl Marx organizes first socialist international. British, French and Dutch fleets attack Japanese in Shimonoseki Straits.	Leo Tolstoy, *War and Peace* (until 1869). Anton Bruckner, *Mass No 1 in D minor.*
1865	In US, Abraham Lincoln assassinated. In Belgium, Leopold I dies; Leopold II becomes king (until 1909).	Lewis Carroll, *Alice's Adventures in Wonderland.*
1866	Austro-Prussian War. Austro-Italian War. In Canada, Fenian 'invasion'.	Friedrich Smetana, *The Bartered Bride.*

Year	Age	Life
1867	46	15 February second marriage to Anna Snitkina. 14 April newly-weds go abroad to avoid creditors. Dresden, Baden and Geneva.
1868	47	Publishes *The Idiot*. Death of 3-month-old Sonia. Transfer to Vevey, then to Milan. Winter in Florence.
1869	48	Return to Dresden. Birth of daughter Liuba. Plans *The Devils*. Learns of Nechaev and murder of Ivanov.
1870	49	Publishes *An Eternal Husband*.
1871		8 July returns to St Petersburg. Birth of son Fedia. Begins publishing *The Devils*.
1872	50	Holiday home in Staraia Russa. Completes *The Devils*.
1873	51	Becomes editor of *The Citizen*. Begins *The Diary of a Writer*.
1874	52	Resigns editorship. Has treatment for emphysema in Ems. Plans *An Accidental Family* (*Podrostok*).
1875	53	*An Accidental Family* published. Again in Ems for treatment.
1876	54	Independent publication of the *Diary,* containing *A Gentle Girl*. Again in Ems.
1877	55	Publishes *The Dream of a Foolish Young Man* in the *Diary*. Death of Nekrasov.
1878	56	Embarks on final novel *The Brothers Karamazov*. 3-year-old son Aleksei dies of epilepsy.
1879	57	Serial publication of *The Brothers Karamazov*. Last visit to Ems for treatment.
1880	58	June speech in Moscow at unveiling of Pushkin memorial. Completion of *The Brothers Karamazov*.
1881	59	28 January dies. 1 February interred in Alexander Nevsky Lavra, St Petersburg.

Year	History	Culture
1867	Prussia forms North German Confederation. Austria forms Austro-Hungarian empire.	Marx, *Das Kapital.* Henrik Ibsen, *Peer Gynt.*
1868	In Britain, William Gladstone becomes prime minister (until 1874). In Japan, Meiji dynasty restored.	Johannes Brahms, *A German Requiem.* W Collins, *The Moonstone.*
1869	Suez Canal opens. Dimitry Mendeleev expounds his periodic law for the classification of the elements.	
1870	Franco-Prussian War. Papal Rome annexed by Italy.	Clément Delibes, *Coppélia.*
1871	At Versailles, William I proclaimed German emperor. In France, Third Republic loses Alsace-Lorraine to Germany.	Verdi, *Aïda.* Caroll, *Through the Looking-Glass.*
1872	In Philippines, rebellion against Spain. First International Association football match.	Thomas Hardy, *Under the Greenwood Tree.*
1873	In Spain, Amadeo I abdicates; republic proclaimed.	Arthur Rimbaud, *A Season in Hell.*
1874	In Britain, Benjamin Disraeli becomes prime minister.	Smetana, *My Fatherland.* J Strauss, *Die Fledermaus.* In Paris, first Impressionist exhibition.
1875	Russo-Japanese agreement over Sakhalin and the Kuriles.	Tchaikovsky, *First Piano Concerto in B-flat minor.* Georges Bizet, *Carmen.*
1876	China declares Korea an independent state. Turkish massacre of Bulgarians. Battle of Little Bighorn; General Custer dies.	Johannes Brahms, *First Symphony.* Wagner, *Siegfried.*
1877	Queen Victoria proclaimed empress of India. Russo-Turkish War. Britain annexes Transvaal.	Emile Zola, *L'Assommoir.*
1878	Congress of Berlin resolves Balkan crisis. Serbia becomes independent. Second Anglo-Afghan War (until 1879).	Tchaikovsky, *Swan Lake.*
1879	Germany and Austria-Hungary form Dual Alliance. In Africa, Zulu War.	Tchaikovsky, *Eugene Onegin.* Ibsen, *The Doll's House.* August Strindberg, *The Red Room.*
1880	In Britain, William Gladstone becomes prime minister. First Boer War (until 1881). Louis Pasteur discovers streptococcus.	Tchaikovsky, *1812 Overture.*
1881	In Russia, Alexander II assassinated. In Japan, political parties established. Tunisia becomes French protectorate. In Algeria, revolt against the French. In Sudan, Mahdi Holy War (until 1898). In eastern Europe, Jewish pogroms.	Jacques Offenbach, *The Tales of Hoffmann.* Anatole France, *Le Crime de Sylvestre Bonnard.* Henry James, *Portrait of Lady.* Ibsen, *Ghosts.*

Further Reading

This guide to Further Reading does not include works mentioned in the Preface or the Notes. For a fuller guide see W J Leatherbarrow, *Fedor Dostoevsky: A Reference Guide* (Boston: G K Hall, 1990).

GENERAL WORKS

Catteau, Jacques, *Dostoyevsky and the Process of Literary Creation* (Cambridge University Press, 1989).

Dowler, Wayne, *Dostoevsky, Grigor'ev and Native Soil Conservatism* (Toronto University Press, 1982).

Fanger, Donald, *Dostoevsky and Romantic Realism: A Study of Dostoevsky in Relation to Balzac, Dickens and Gogol* (Harvard University Press, 1965).

Gibson, A Boyce, *The Religion of Dostoevsky* (London: SCM Press, 1973).

Holquist, J M, *Dostoevsky and the Novel* (Princeton University Press, 1977).

Jackson, Robert Louis, *The Art of Dostoevsky: Deliriums and Nocturnes* (Princeton University Press, 1987).

Jones, John, *Dostoevsky* (Oxford University Press, 1983).

Jones, Malcolm V, *Dostoevsky: The Novel of Discord* (London: Elek, 1976).

De Jonge, A, *Dostoevsky and the Age of Intensity* (London: Secker and Warburg, 1975).

Kjetsaa, Geir, *Fyodor Dostoevsky: A Writer's Life* (London: Macmillan, 1988).

Knapp, Liza, *The Annihilation of Inertia: Dostoevsky and Metaphysics* (Northwestern University Press, 1996).

Leatherbarrow, W J, *Fedor Dostoevsky* (Boston: Twayne, 1981).

Leatherbarrow, W J, (ed.) *The Cambridge Companion to Dostoevskii* (Cambridge University Press, 2002).

Morson, Gary Saul, *The Boundaries of Genre: Dostoevsky's* The Diary of a Writer *and the Traditions of Literary Utopia* (Texas University Press, 1981).

Morson, Gary Saul, *Narrative and Freedom: The Shadows of Time* (Yale University Press, 1994).
Pattison, George, and Thompson, Diane Oenning (eds.) *Dostoevsky and the Christian Tradition* (Cambridge University Press, 2001).
Steiner, George, *Tolstoy or Dostoevsky? An Essay in the Old Criticism* (London: Faber and Faber, 1959).
Straus, Nina Pelikan, *Dostoevsky and the Woman Question: Rereadings at the end of a Century* (New York: St Martin's Press, 1994).
Terras, Victor, *Reading Dostoevsky* (Wisconsin University Press, 1998).
Wasiolek, Edward, *Dostoevsky: The Major Fiction* (Cambridge, Mass.: MIT Press, 1964).
Wellek, Rene (ed.), *Dostoevsky: A Collection of Critical Essays* (Englewood Cliffs, NJ: Prentice Hall, 1962).

ON *CRIME AND PUNISHMENT*

Freeborn, Richard, Ch. 7 in *The Rise of the Russian Novel* (Cambridge University Press, 1973).
Gibian, George, *Feodor Dostoevsky, Crime and Punishment* (New York: Norton, 1974).
Jackson, Robert Louis (ed.), *Twentieth-Century Interpretations of* Crime and Punishment*: A Collection of Critical Essays* (Englewood Cliffs, NJ: Prentice Hall, 1974).
Rosenshield, Gary, Crime and Punishment*: Techniques of the Omniscient Author* (Lisse: Peter de Ridder, 1978).

ON *THE IDIOT*

Dalton, Elizabeth, *Unconscious Structure in* The Idiot*: A Study in Literature and Psycholanalysis* (Princeton University Press, 1979).
Miller, Robin Feuer, *Dostoevsky and* The Idiot*: Author, Narrator and Reader* (Harvard University Press, 1981).
Slattery, D P, The Idiot*: Dostoevsky's Fantastic Prince: A Phenomenological Approach* (Berne and New York: Lang, 1983).
Terras, Victor, The Idiot*: An Interpretation* (Boston: Twayne, 1990).
Wasiolek, Edward (ed.), *Fyodor Dostoevsky: The Notebooks for* The Idiot, trans. Katherine Strelsky (Chicago University Press, 1967).

ON *THE DEVILS*

Leatherbarrow, W J, *Dostoevsky's* The Devils*: A Critical Companion* (Northwestern University Press, 1999).

Vladiv, S V, *Narrative Principles in Dostoevsky's* Besy*: A Structural Analysis* (Lang, 1979).

Wasiolek, Edward (ed.), *Fyodor Dostoevsky: The Notebooks for* The Possessed, trans. Victor Terras (Chicago University Press, 1968).

ON *THE BROTHERS KARAMAZOV*

Belknap, Robert, *The Genesis of* The Brothers Karamazov*: The Aesthetics, Ideology and Psychology of Making a Text* (Northwestern University Press, 1990).

Dunlop, J B, *Staretz Amvrosy: Model for Dostoevsky's Staretz Zossima* (Belmont, Mass, 1972).

Leatherbarrow, W J, *Dostoyevsky:* The Brothers Karamazov (Cambridge University Press, 1992).

Linner, Sven, *Starets Zosima in* The Brothers Karamazov (Stockholm: Almquist and Wiksell, 1975).

Matlaw, Ralph, The Brothers Karamazov*: Novelistic Techniques* (The Hague: Mouton, 1967).

Miller, Robin Feuer, The Brothers Karamazov*: Worlds of the Novel* (Boston: Twayne, 1992).

Perlina, Nina, *Varieties of Poetic Utterance: Quotation in* The Brothers Karamazov (Lanham: America University Press, 1985).

Sandoz, Ellis, *Political Apocalypse: A Study of Dostoevsky's Grand Inquisitor* (Louisiana State University Press, 1971).

Sutherland, Stewart R, *Atheism and the Rejection of God: Contemporary Philosophy and* The Brothers Karamazov (Oxford: Blackwell, 1977).

Wasiolek, Edward (ed.), *Fyodor Dostoevsky: The Notebooks for* The Brothers Karamazov, trans. Victor Terras (Chicago University Press, 1971).

Picture Sources

The author and publishers wish to express their thanks to the following sources of illustrative material and/or permission to reproduce it. They will make the proper acknowledgements in future editions in the event that any omissions have occurred.

Anne Ronan Picture Library: pp. 3, 11, 28, 30, 41, 49, 56, 120. Heritage Image Pictures: pp. 22, 27, 35, 37, 45, 67, 80, 134, 135. Mary Evans Picture Library: pp. 22, 109. The Alexander Pushkin State Museum, Moscow: p.131. RIA Novosti: pp. 2, 5, 7, 16, 93, 136. The Heirs of Boris Smelov, St Petersburg: pp.15, 21, 91. The Russian State Library, Moscow: pp. 70, 105, 123. Topham Picturepoint: pp. 4, 9, 24, 33, 42, 57, 77, 99, 110, 113, 117, 124, 129, 132.

Index

Alei (Tatar), 39
Alexander I, Tsar, 4; death, 7
Alexander II, Tsar, 133; attempted assassination, 76, 97, 122; assassination, 97, 109, 134
Alexander III, Tsar, 109
Ambrose, Father, 120
anarchism, 54
atheism, 83, 92
Austen, Jane, 14

Bad Homburg, 58, 81
Baden-Baden, 57, 81–2
Bakhtin, Mikhail, 33
Bakunin, Mikhail, 54, 97; biography, 54
Balkans, 6
Balzac, Honoré de, 17, 24; *Eugénie Grandet*, 24
Basel, 83
Beketov, Aleksei, 29
Belinsky, Vissarion Grigorevich, 22–3, 25, 26, 48, 83, 95, 96, 98; utopian socialism, 28–9; Dostoevsky's reminiscences, 111; *Letter to Gogol*, 31–2
Bell, The, 54
Berlin, 53, 81
Bible, 12
Blanc, Louis, 30, 31
Bologna, 93
Borodino, battle of, 11
Brown, Martha, 64
Butashevich-Petrashevsky, Mikhail, 30, 35
Byron, Lord, 5; *Don Juan*, 9
Byronism, 9, 22
Byzantium, 96

Caucasus, 6
censorship, 23, 38, 47, 54, 55, 61, 110, 112
Chaadaev, P Ia, 95, 114; biography, 96; *Apology of a Madman*, 96; *Philosophical Letter*, 96
Chekhov, Anton, 3
Chermak boarding school, 14
Chermashnia, 118
Chernyshevsky, Nikolai, 46–7, 60; arrested, 52–3, 55; 'The Aesthetic Relations of Art to Reality', 47; *What is to be Done?*, 55
children, 117
Christ, 13, 28–9, 39–40, 48, 61, 83–4, 118, 125–6; Holbein's, 83, 89
Christianity, 96, 121
Citizen, The, 109–10, 112
Classicism, 8
Congress of Peace and Freedom, 83
Constantine, Grand-Duke, 7, 130
Contemporary, The, 29, 46, 49, 52, 55; closed, 77
Copenhagen, 66

Corneille, Pierre, 17
corporal punishment, 32
crime novel, 135
Crimean War, 6, 41, 42, 46, 48, 98

Darovoe, 12, 18, 118
Darwinism, 89
Dawn, 92, 95
Decembrist Revolt, 6–8, 10 38
Dickens, Charles: *The Old Curiosity Shop*, 50; *The Pickwick Papers*, 133; *see also* Micawber, Mr; Pickwick, Mr
dictation, 77, 78
'dictatorship of the heart', 130
Dobroliubov, Nikolai, 46–7; *What is Oblomovism?*, 46
Don Quixote, 84
Dostoevsky, Aleksei, 19
Dostoevsky, Alesha, 117; death, 120
Dostoevsky, Alexandra, 11
Dostoevsky, Andrei, 11
Dostoevsky, Dr Mikhail, 11–12; short temper, 12; admitted to nobility, 12; death, 18–19
Dostoevsky, Fedor (son), 108
Dostoevsky, Fedor Mikhailovich: birth, 3, 10–11; childhood, 11–15; father–son relationship, 12; religion, 12–13, 28–9, 39–40; belief in Russian national identity, 13; education, 14; studies at Academy for Engineers, 15–16, 23–4; letters to his brother, 16–19, 27, 36; money problems, 16–17, 55, 63–6, 81, 85, 92, 94, 109, 120, 136; talent for drawing, 17; vision of humanity, 17; effect of father's death, 18–19; epilepsy, 18–19, 30, 38, 42, 55, 67, 81, 93, 95, 112, 117, 120, 136; purpose as writer, 19; style, 22, 33, 34, 50, 94; translates *Eugénie Grandet*, 24; privacy, 24, 39; sense of inferiority, 27; rivalries, 27, 92, 130; politics, 27–9, 30–2, 98–100, 109, 119, 122, 130; rift with Belinsky, 29; reads Belinsky's *Letter to Gogol*, 31–2, 34–5; arrested, 34; death sentence, 35; penal servitude, 36–40; confession of faith, 39–40; relationship and marriage with Marsha Isaeva, 41–2, 44, 56, 62; restored to nobility, 42; patriotism, 45, 100, 132; return to St Petersburg from exile, 46, 47; belief in freedom, 47; travels abroad, 53–5, 56–8, 64–6, 81–5, 92–3, 112, 118, 130; relationship with Polina Suslova, 56–8, 65; gambling, 56–8, 64–5, 81, 108; brother's and wife's death, 63; relationships with Martha Brown and Anna Korvin-Krukovskaia, 64; relationship and marriage with Anna Snitkina, 77, 79, 80–1, 136; quarrel with Turgenev, 82; first daughter dies, 84; police surveillance, 85, 130; second daughter born, 93; work routine, 93–4; stops gambling, 108; son born, 108; gains influence, 109; celebrity, 112, 117, 133; public readings, 112, 117, 120; emphysema, 112, 117, 130; second son born, 117; member of the

Academy of Sciences, 117; death of son, 120; speech at unveiling of Pushkin's statue, 130–3; vision of Russian destiny, 132; death, 133; funeral, 134
WORKS: *An Accidental Family*, 14, 113–16; *Bobok*, 111; *The Brothers Karamzov*, 44, 58, 89, 118–29, 130, 135; *Crime and Punishment*, 15, 65–76, 79, 80, 95, 135; 'The Crocodile', 62; *The Devils*, 93, 94, 97–107, 108, 109, 110, 135; *The Diary of a Writer*, 13, 110–11, 117, 118, 122, 130, 133; *The Double*, 26–7, 51; *The Dream of a Foolish Young Man*, 111–12; *Drunkards*, 64, 66, 69; *An Eternal Husband*, 93, 94–5; *The Gambler*, 77–8; *A Gentle Girl*, 111; *The Idiot*, 58, 64, 85–91, 92; *The Insulted and Injured*, 49, 50–2; 'The Landlady', 32; *The Life of a Great Sinner*, 92; 'A Little Hero', 34, 43; *Memoirs from the House of the Dead*, 38, 49, 56; 'Mr Prokharchin', 33; 'My Acquaintance with Belinsky', 83; 'A Nasty Story', 62; *Netochka Nezvanova*, 33–4; *Notes from Underground*, 58–62; *Poor Folk*, 24–6, 33, 118; 'Uncle's Dream', 43–4; 'The Village of Stepanchikovo', 43, 44; 'A Weak Heart', 33; 'White Nights', 32; *Winter Notes of Summer Impressions*, 53
Dostoevsky, Liubov (Liuba, Lalia), 93
Dostoevsky, Maria, 11; interest in her children, 12–13; death, 15, 18
Dostoevsky, Mikhail, 11, 14, 47, 49, 55; enters Tallinn academy, 16; death, 63
Dostoevsky, Nikolai, 11
Dostoevsky, Sonia (daughter), 84–5
Dostoevsky, Sonia (niece), 94
Dostoevsky, Vera, 11
Dostoevsky museum, 12
Dresden, 81, 93
Druzhakov (teacher), 14

Ems, 112, 118, 130
Epoch, 58, 59, 63, 64
'epoch of great endeavours', 109

farce, 43
Fatherland Notes, 23, 43, 114
'Fathers, the', 46, 48
Fedorov, N F, 119
Feuerbach, Ludwig Andreas, 28, 29
Florence, 54, 85, 92
Fonzivina, Natalia, 38, 39, 61
Fourier, Charles, 30, 31
Franco–Prussian War, 95
Frank, Joseph, 83
French Revolution, 41
Freud, Sigmund, 18–19

Gaskell, Elizabeth: *Mary Barton*, 49
generational conflict, 117, 118
Geneva, 83, 84, 97
Genoa, 54
'Godmanhood', 118
Goethe, Johann Wolfgang von, 17
Gogol, Nikolay Vasilievich, 22–3, 25, 26, 43, 131; humour, 27; ridiculed, 44; *Dead Souls*, 22–3; *Selected Passages from a Correspondence*

with Friends, 31–2, 44
Goncharov, Ivan, *Oblomov*, 46
Gothic, 14, 26, 135
Grigoriev, Apollon, 63
Grigorovich (writer), 24

Hegel, Georg Wilhelm Friedrich, 28, 40
Herodotus, 40
Herzen, Alexander, 54, 58, 83, 114; biography, 54; Dostoevsky's reminiscences, 111; *Past and Thoughts*, 54
Hoffmann, E T W, 17
Holbein, Hans, the Younger, 83, 86, 89
Hugo, Victor, 17, 119
Humboldt, Alexander, Baron von, 3

Ilinsky (patricide), 119
Industrial Revolution, 5
intelligentsia 6, 13–14, 28, 45–6, 48, 54, 92, 95, 98, 101, 108
Isaeva, Maria (Marsha), 41–2, 62; tuberculosis, 56, 58; death, 61, 63
Italy, 54, 57, 85
Ivanov (murdered revolutionary), 96, 97, 105
Ivanova, Sonia, 84

James, Henry, 76, 85–6, 94
Job, 28

Kant, Immanuel, 40
Karakozov, Dmitri, 76–7, 97, 122
Katkov, Mikhail Nikiforovich, 65–7, 76, 83, 97, 98, 106, 114, 120
Kepler, Johannes, 73
Koni, A F, 119
Koran, 40
Korvin-Krukovskaia, Anna, 64
Kraevsky, A A, 23, 29, 43, 64
Kursk, 118
Kuznetsk, 41–2
Latin, 12
Lenin, Vladimir Ilich, 55
Lermontov, Mikhail Yur'evich, 22–3; *A Hero of Our Times*, 22
Leskov, Nikolai, *Lady Macbeth of Mtsensk*, 63
Literary Fund, 56, 130
literature: confessional 25; 'natural school', 26; prison, 38; Russian, 8–10, 14, 22–3, 45–7; *see also* crime novel
London, 53–4; Crystal Palace, 55
Loris-Melikov, Mikhail Tarielovich, 130
Lycurgus, 73

Mahomet, 73
Maikov, Apollon, 81, 84, 85, 94, 98
Maikov, Valerian, 29; death, 29
Marei (peasant), 13
'men of the 40s', 28, 45, 54
Meshchersky, Prince, 109, 110, 112
Micawber, Mr (Dickens), 95
Milan, 85
Moscow, 4, 58, 130; Hospital for the Poor, 11, 12, 15; Petrovsky Agricultural Academy, 94, 96, 97

Naples, 58
Napoleon Bonaparte, 4, 73; invasion of Russia, 4, 11
Nechaev, Sergei, 96–7, 98, 103;

biography, 97; *The Catechism of a Revolutionary*, 97
Nekrasov, Nikolai, 25, 49, 114; death, 118
Neva River, 8, 20
New Testament, 38
Newton, Isaac, 73
Nicholas I, Tsar, 7–8, 36; plots against, 31; permits Dostoevsky's promotion, 42
nihilism, 52, 59, 67, 76, 83, 86, 92
Novgorod, 109
Nurra, Lezgin, 39

Ogarev, Nikolay Platonovich, 83
Omsk, 37, 40
Optina Pustyn', 120
Orlov (mass murderer), 38
Orthodox Church, 5, 32, 48
Ostrovsky, Alexander, 49

Palm-Durov circle, 31, 32, 34
Panaeva, Madame, 27
Panslavism, 108
Paris, 4, 53, 56–8, 82, 119; 1848 revolution, 32, 54
Pascal, Blaise, 17
Pasha (stepson), 44, 81
patricide, 18–19, 118, 119
peasantry, 47–8, 54, 108
peasants, 6, 13, 15, 18, 31; convicts, 37–9; unrest, 52
People's Will, 108, 122, 130, 134
Perov (painter), 112
Peter the Great, Tsar, 4, 20, 96
Peterson, N P, 119
Petrashevsky circle, 30–1, 33, 34, 39
Pickwick, Mr (Dickens), 84
Pisarev, Dmitri, 59, 67
Plutarch, 40
Pobedonostsev (tutor), 109
pochvennichestvo (philosophy of the soil), 13, 48, 49
Populism, 108–9
Prague, 93
prostitutes, 53
Proudhon, Pierre-Joseph, 30, 31
Pushkin, Alexander, 8–10, 14, 87; biography, 9; unveiling of statue, 130–3; *Boris Godunov*, 9, 24; *Eugene Onegin*, 9–10, 132; 'The Gypsies', 9, 132; 'The Prisoner of the Caucasus', 9

Racine, Jean, 17
Radcliffe, Ann, 14
realism, 128, 133, 135
Roman Catholicism, 90, 96
Romanticism, 5, 8–10, 16, 18, 28, 135
Russia, 4–6, 135; Napoleonic invasion, 4, 11; relations with Europe, 4, 48, 82, 92, 96, 98, 123; reform, 6, 10; rural world, 10; spirit of, 14; subjection to imperial power, 16; European, 36, 37, 44–5; spiritual superiority, 45, 82, 84; Polish uprising against, 55; Soviet, 104; in 1870s, 108; Holy Synod, 109; destiny, 132; relations with Asia, 133
Russian empire, 3–5
Russian Messenger, The, 65, 67, 76, 83, 120
Russian Word, The, 58, 59
Russo–Turkish War, 109

St Petersburg, 7, 15–16, 20–1, 23, 24; urban mystery, 20–1; Balzac visits, 24; literary society, 27, 29, 120; outbreak of fires, 52; money-lenders, 64; depicted in *Crime and Punishment*, 75–6
Academy for Engineers, 15–16, 23–4, 29, 42; Alexander Nevsky Lavra, 134; Izmailovsky Cathedral, 80; Peter and Paul Fortress, 34–5, 43, 97; Semenovsky Square, 35; Senate Square, 7; Summer Gardens, 76
Saltykov, Mikhail, 49
Salvador (Polina's lover), 57
Sand, George, 17
Schelling, Friedrich W J, 28
Schiller, Friedrich von, 14; *Maria Stuart*, 14, 24; *The Robbers*, 14
Schopenhauer, Arthur, 57
Semipalatinsk, 40, 42, 43, 66
Sentimentalism, 8
serfdom, 5–6, 23, 32
serfs, 6, 23, 31; emancipation of, 6, 46–7, 52, 54
Sevastopol, 42
Shakespeare, William, 17
Shidlovsky, Ivan, 16
Siberia, 13, 44, 54; Dostoevsky's exile, 36, 43, 66
skandal scenes, 26, 43, 104
Slavophilism, 48
Snitkin, Ivan, 94, 97
Snitkina, Anna Grigorievna, 77, 79, 80–1, 83–5, 92–3, 108, 133; first daughter dies, 84; second daughter born, 93; son born, 108; dedicatee of *The Brothers Karamzov*, 122; granted pension, 133
socialism, 28–9, 31, 54, 55, 97, 100, 124
Solon, 73
Solovev, Vladimir, 118–19, 120, 124, 134
'Sons, the', 46, 48, 101
Soviet Union, 32
Speshnev, Nikolai, 31, 32
Stalinism, 104
Staraia Russa, 109, 118
Stellovsky (publisher), 64, 77, 78, 95
Stirner, Max, 28
Strakhov, (writer and friend), 54, 55, 94
suicide, 111–12, 114
'superfluous men', 23, 45, 60
Suslova, Polina, 56–8, 65, 81

Taganrog, 7
Tallinn, 16
terrorism, 108, 109, 122, 130
Third Department, 8
Time, 20, 47, 48, 49, 54, 55
Tolstoy, Count Leo Nikolaevich, biography, 3; style, 22; rivalry with Dostoevsky, 92; *Anna Karenina*, 3, 114; *War and Peace*, 3, 92, 96, 100, 115
Totleben, Eduard Ivanovich, 42
Trepov, General, 119
Trieste, 93
Tula, 12, 13, 18
Turgenev, Ivan, 22, 27, 45–7, 63, 82, 94, 95; rivalry with Dostoevsky, 27, 130; Dostoevsky visits, 57–8, 82; loan to

Dostoevsky, 65, 82, 120; Dostoevsky quarrels with, 82; atheism, 83; caricatured, 104; speech at unveiling of Pushkin's statue, 130–1; *The Diary of a Superfluous Man*, 60; *Enough*, 104; *Fathers and Sons*, 52, 57, 59; *Home of the Gentry*, 45–6; *On the Eve*, 46; *Phantoms*, 57, 58; *Rudin*, 45; *Sketches from a Hunter's Album*, 45; *Smoke*, 82
Turin, 54
Tver, 45, 100

Venice, 93
Vevey, 84–5
Viardot, Pauline, 57
Vladimir, 58
Voltaire, 125

Waterloo, battle of, 4
Wiesbaden, 56, 65, 66, 108
Wrangel, Baron, 41, 63, 66

xenophobia, 81, 90

Yanishev, Father, 66
Young Russia (leaflet), 52

Zasulich, Vera, 119, 122

About the author

Richard Freeborn, MA DPhil DLitt, is Emeritus Professor of Russian Literature at the University of London. He is the author of *Turgenev: The Novelist's Novelist*, *A Short History of Modern Russia*, *The Rise of the Russian Novel* and *The Russian Revolutionary Novel*.

He has contributed to *The Cambridge History of Russian Literature*, *The Age of Realism*, *Encyclopedia of the Novel*, *Reference Guide to Russian Literature* and *The Cambridge Companion to Tolstoy* and has co-edited *Russian Literary Attitudes from Pushkin to Solzhenitsyn*, *Russian and Slavic Literature* and *Ideology in Russian Literature*.

He has translated several works by Ivan Turgenev, including *Sketches from a Hunter's Album*, *First Love and Other Stories*, *A Month in the Country* and *Fathers and Sons*, as well as Dostoevsky's *An Accidental Family*. Richard Freeborn has also written four novels: *Two Ways of Life*, *The Emigration of Sergey Ivanovich*, *Russian Roulette* and *The Russian Crucifix*.